PUTTING
PEOPLE FIRST

PUTTING
PEOPLE FIRST

*How We Can All
Change America*

Gov. Bill Clinton
Sen. Al Gore

TIMES BOOKS

Contents

Preface

ALL OVER AMERICA, you can hear the voices of change. Traveling across the country, we have listened to those voices and learned from them.

Putting People First is just one result of our continuing conversation with the American people. We have learned that you are hungry for leaders who offer more than empty slogans and thirty-second sound bites. We have tried to respond with the substance you demand—with a vision and a plan for the future. We hope our ideas are only the beginning of a serious debate that you will bring into your homes, workplaces, and communities.

That debate is sorely needed. For the last twelve years, government has served the rich and special interests. Millions of middle-class Americans have paid more to government but gotten less in return. The results have been devastating: record numbers of people without jobs, schools that are failing, millions with inadequate health care, and more dangerous streets and neighborhoods.

It is time for a change, time for leaders willing to accept responsibility and ready to put the power of the presidency to work for the American people.

In the pages that follow, we outline our plan to put people first and fight for what Americans deserve: good jobs, world-class education, quality health care, and safe streets and neighborhoods. It's a plan to unite Americans behind the hope we all share—that we can create a better future for our children.

Our policies are neither liberal nor conservative, neither Democratic nor Republican. They are new. They are different. We are confident they will work.

None of us has all the answers, and no American will agree with every aspect of our plan or every detail of our vision. But we hope every American who hears our ideas will react to them—and that you'll let us know your own thoughts and suggestions. We believe you have a right to know what we'll do and where we stand.

We hope that you will join our campaign to change America and make our great nation everything it was meant to be.

Bill Clinton

Al Gore

PUTTING
PEOPLE FIRST

Putting People First:
A Strategy for Change

DURING THE 1980s, our government betrayed the values that make America great: providing opportunity, taking responsibility, rewarding work. While the rich got richer, the forgotten middle class—the people who work hard and play by the rules—took it on the chin. They paid higher taxes to a government that gave them little in return. Washington failed to put people first. No wonder our nation has compiled its worst economic record in fifty years.

Our political system isn't working either. Washington is dominated by powerful interests and an entrenched bureaucracy. Americans are tired of blame. They are ready for leaders willing to take responsibility.

Our national economic strategy puts people first by investing more than $50 billion each year for the next four years while cutting the deficit in half. These investments will create millions of high-wage jobs and help America compete in the global economy.

Our strategy includes:

• *Putting America to work* by rebuilding our country, converting from a defense to a peacetime economy, revitalizing our cities, encouraging private investment, and opening up world markets.

- *Rewarding work* by providing tax fairness to working families, ending welfare as we know it, providing family leave, and cracking down on deadbeat parents.
- *Supporting lifetime learning* by bringing parents and children together, improving schools, training high school graduates, offering every American the chance to borrow money to go to college and serve our nation, and retraining workers.
- *Providing affordable quality health care* by radically controlling costs, reducing paperwork, phasing in universal access to basic medical coverage, and cracking down on drug manufacturers and insurance companies.
- *Revolutionizing government* by cutting 100,000 federal jobs, eliminating wasteful spending, limiting the power of special interests, stopping the revolving door from public service to private enrichment, and reforming campaign finance and practices.

To pay for our investments and reduce the national deficit, we will save nearly $300 billion by cutting spending, closing corporate tax loopholes, and forcing the very wealthy to pay their fair share of taxes. Our plan will cut the deficit in half within four years and assure that it continues to fall each year after that.

A NATIONAL ECONOMIC STRATEGY

It's time to put people first.

That is the core of our national economic strategy for America. And that will be the fundamental idea that guides our Administration.

America is the greatest nation on earth. But for more than a decade our government has been rigged in favor of the rich and special interests. While the very wealthiest Americans get richer, middle-class Americans pay more taxes to their government and get less in return. Our government has betrayed the values that make us great—providing opportunity, taking responsibility, and rewarding hard work.

For twelve years, the driving idea behind American economic policy has been cutting taxes on the richest individuals and corporations and hoping that their new wealth would "trickle down" to the rest of us.

This policy has failed.

The Republicans in Washington have compiled the worst economic record in fifty years: the slowest economic growth, slowest job growth, and slowest income growth since the Great Depression. During the 1980s the wealthiest 1 percent of Americans got 70 percent of income gains. By the end of the decade, American CEOs were paying themselves 100 times more than their workers. Washington stood by while quick-buck artists brought down the savings-and-loan industry, leaving the rest of us with a $500 billion bill.

While the rich cashed in, the forgotten middle class worked harder for less money and paid more taxes to a government that failed to produce what we need: good jobs in a growing economy, world-class education, affordable health care, and safe streets and neighborhoods. The working poor had the door of opportunity slammed in their face.

A decade ago, Americans earned higher wages than anyone else in the world. Now we're thirteenth, and falling. In Europe and Japan our competitors' economies grew three and four times faster than ours—because their leaders decided to invest in their people and Washington did not.

In the emerging global economy, everything is mobile: capital, factories, even entire industries. The only resource that's really rooted in a nation—and the ultimate source of all its wealth—is its people. The only way America can compete and win in the twenty-first century is to have the best-educated, best-trained workforce in the world, linked together by transportation and communication networks second to none.

We believe in free enterprise and the power of market forces. We know economic growth will be the best jobs program we'll ever have. But economic growth does not come without a national economic strategy to invest in people and meet the competition. Today we have no economic vision, no economic leadership, and no economic strategy.

Our political system has failed us, too. Washington is dominated by powerful interests and an entrenched bureaucracy. Too many public officials enter the revolving door and emerge as high-priced influence peddlers. Too often those we elect to lead seem to respond more quickly to special interests than to the real problems of real people.

No wonder all of us have had enough. Our government doesn't work. People who pay the bills get little value for their dollar and have no voice in Washington. They are tired of hearing politicians blame each other. They are eager for someone to take responsibility and ready for leaders who will challenge all of us again.

But we will reach our goals only if we focus on our country's greatest resource. That is why putting people first is the heart and soul of our national economic strategy—and the key to the American future.

Our strategy puts people first by investing more than $50 billion each year over the next four years to put America back to work—the most dramatic economic growth program since the Second World War. Our strategy recognizes that the only way to lay the foundation for renewed American prosperity is to spur both public and private investment. To reclaim our future, we must strive to close both the budget deficit and the investment gap.

These investments will create millions of high-wage jobs and provide tax relief to working families. They will also help move people from welfare to work, provide lifetime learning, and ensure affordable health care for every citizen.

To pay for these investments and reduce our national deficit, we will save nearly $300 billion by cutting spending, closing corporate tax loopholes, and requiring the very wealthy to pay their fair share of taxes. Our plan will cut the deficit in half within four years and assure that it continues to fall each year after that.

PUTTING AMERICA TO WORK

Putting people first demands, above all, that we put America back to work.

For the last twelve years Washington has penalized hard work and sold out American families. As the recession sends working families into poverty, the Republicans throw up their hands instead of rolling up their sleeves.

The results have been devastating. Record numbers of Americans are unemployed and millions more must settle for insecure, low-wage, no-benefit jobs. Small businesses—which create most of the new jobs in this country—are starved for capital and credit. Washington continues to grant tax deductions for outrageous executive pay and reward American corporations that move their plants and jobs overseas.

The corrupt do-nothing values of the 1980s must never mislead us again. Never again should Washington reward those who speculate in paper, instead of those who put people first. Never again should we sit idly by while the plight of hardworking Americans is ignored. Never again should we pass on our debts to our children while their futures silently slip through our fingers.

Our national economic strategy will reward the people who work hard creating new jobs, starting new businesses, and investing in our people and our plants here at home. To restore economic growth, we need to help free enterprise flourish, put our people back to work, and learn again how to compete. Our plan will:

Shut the Door on the "Something for Nothing" Decade. We can do this by:

• Making the wealthiest Americans pay their fair share in taxes,

• Ending tax breaks for American companies that shut down their plants here and ship American jobs overseas,

- Eliminating deductions for outrageous executive pay, and
- Cracking down on foreign companies that prosper here and manipulate tax laws to their advantage.

Rebuild America. The 1980s saw the concrete foundations of the United States crumble as the investment gap widened between America and our global competitors. By the decade's end, Japan and Germany were investing more than twelve times what we spend on roads, bridges, sewers, and the information networks and technologies of the future. No wonder they threaten to surpass America in manufacturing by 1996. No wonder we are slipping behind.

To create millions of high-wage jobs and smooth our transition from a defense to a peacetime economy, we will rebuild America and develop the world's best communication, transportation, and environmental systems.

As a prominent part of our strategy to put people first, we will create a Rebuild America Fund, with a $20 billion federal investment each year for the next four years, leveraged with state, local, private sector, and pension fund contributions. User fees such as road tolls and solid-waste disposal charges will help guarantee these investments.

Just as constructing interstate highways in the 1950s ushered in two decades of unparalleled growth, creating the pathways of the twenty-first century will help put Americans back to work and spur economic growth. States and localities will be responsible for project development and management. The creation of large, predictable markets will stimulate private industry to invest in our economy and create new high-wage jobs.

We will focus on four critical areas:

• Transportation. This will include renovation of our country's roads, bridges, and railroads; creation of a high-speed rail network linking our major cities and commercial hubs; investment in "smart" highway technology to expand the capacity, speed, and efficiency of our major roadways; and development of high-tech short-haul aircraft.

• A national information network to link every home, business, lab, classroom, and library by the year 2015. To expand access to information, we will put public records, databases, libraries, and educational materials on line for public use.

• Environmental technology to create the world's most advanced systems to recycle, treat toxic waste, and clean our air and water; this technology can also develop new, clean energy sources. We need not make a false choice between protecting our environment and spurring economic growth.

• Defense conversion to ensure that the communities and millions of talented workers that won the Cold War don't get left out in the cold. Many of the skills and technologies required to rebuild America are similar to those now used in our defense industries. We will encourage companies that bid on projects to rebuild America to contract work to, or purchase, existing defense facilities; order the Pentagon to conduct a national defense-jobs inventory to assist displaced workers; and provide special conversion loans and grants to small business defense contractors.

Invest in Communities. While America's great cities fall into disrepair, Washington continues to ignore their fate. Private enterprise has abandoned our cities, leaving our young people with few job prospects and less hope. To restore urban economic vitality and bring back high-paying jobs to our cities, we will:

• Target funding and Community Development Block Grants to rebuild America's urban roads, bridges, water and sewage-treatment plants, and low-income housing stock, stressing "ready to go" projects. Require companies that bid on these projects to set up a portion of their operations in low-income neighborhoods and employ local residents.

• Create a nationwide network of community development banks to provide small loans to low-income entrepreneurs and homeowners in the inner cities. These banks will also provide advice and assistance to entrepreneurs, invest in affordable housing, and help mobilize private lenders.

• Fight crime by putting 100,000 new police officers on the streets. We will create a National Police Corps and offer unemployed veterans and active military personnel a chance to become law enforcement officers here at home. We will also expand community policing, fund more drug treatment, and establish community "boot camps" to discipline first-time nonviolent offenders.

• Create urban enterprise zones in stagnant inner cities, but only for companies willing to take responsibility. Business taxes and federal regulations will be minimized to provide incentives to set up shop. In return, companies will have to make jobs for local residents a top priority.

• Ease the credit crunch in our inner cities by passing a more progressive Community Reinvestment Act to prevent redlining, and by requiring financial institutions to invest in their communities.

Encourage Private Investment in America. Ten years ago, the United States spent about $400 more per person than Japan in capital investment. Today the Japanese invest more than twice as much in their nation as we do in ours. We must either change our course or continue to slide.

To help American business create new jobs and compete in the global economy, we must dramatically increase private investment. Our plan would:

• Provide a targeted investment tax credit to encourage investment in the new plants and productive equipment here at home that we need to compete in the global economy.

• Help small businesses and entrepreneurs by offering a 50 percent tax exclusion to those who take risks by making long-term investments in new businesses.

• Make permanent the research and development tax credit to reward companies that invest in groundbreaking technologies.

• Create a civilian research and development agency to bring together businesses and universities to develop cutting-edge products and technologies. This agency will increase our commercial research and development spending, focusing its efforts in crucial new industries such as biotechnology, robotics, high-speed computing, and environmental technology.

Open Up World Markets. Because every $1 billion of increased American exports will create 20,000 to 30,000 new jobs, we will move aggressively to open foreign markets to quality American goods and services. We will urge our trading partners in Europe and the Pacific Rim to abandon unfair trade subsidies in key sectors like shipbuilding and aerospace—and act swiftly if they fail to respond. To ensure a more level playing field, we will:

• Pass a stronger, sharper "Super 301" trade bill: if other nations refuse to play by our trade rules, we'll play by theirs.

• Support a free trade agreement with Mexico so long as it provides adequate protection for workers, farmers, and the environment on both sides of the border.

• Create an Economic Security Council, similar to the National Security Council, with responsibility for coordinating America's international economic policy.

• Reform the office of the U.S. Trade Representative by issuing an executive order banning trade negotiators from cashing in on their positions by later becoming lobbyists for foreign governments or corporations. We must transform this office into a corps of trade experts whose primary aim is to serve their country, not sell out for lucrative paychecks from foreign competitors.

REWARDING WORK AND FAMILIES

Putting our people first means honoring and rewarding those who work hard and play by the rules. It means recognizing that government doesn't raise children—people do. It means that we must reward work, demand responsibility, and end welfare as we know it.

Washington has abandoned working families. Millions of Americans are running harder and harder just to stay in place. While taxes fall and incomes rise for those at the top of the totem pole, middle-class families pay more and earn less. Wages are flat, good jobs have become scarce, and poverty has exploded. Health-care costs have skyrocketed, and millions have seen their health benefits disappear.

Today almost one of every five people who works full-time doesn't earn enough to support his or her family above the poverty line. Deadbeat parents owe $25 billion in unpaid child support and have left millions of single-parent families in poverty.

In the 1980s the Republicans used welfare as a wedge to divide Americans against each other. They silently hacked away at the programs that keep disadvantaged children healthy and prepare them for school. They talked about "family values," but increased the burden on American families.

Our national economic strategy will strengthen families and empower all Americans to work. It will break the cycle of dependency and end welfare as we know it. It includes:

Expanding the Earned Income Tax Credit. To ensure that no one with a family who works full-time has to raise children in poverty, we will increase the Earned Income Tax Credit to make up the difference between a family's earnings and the poverty level. The credit will also be expanded for part-time workers, giving them a greater incentive to work.

Middle-class Tax Fairness. We will lower the tax burden on middle-class Americans by asking the very wealthy to pay their fair share. Middle-class taxpayers will have a choice between a children's tax credit or a significant reduction in their income tax rate. Virtually every industrialized nation recognizes the importance of strong families in its tax code; we should, too.

Welfare-to-Work. We will scrap the current welfare system and make welfare a second chance, not a way of life. We will empower people on welfare with the education, training, and child care they need for up to two years, so they can break the cycle of dependency. After that, those who can work will have to go to work, either by taking a job in the private sector or through community service.

Family and Medical Leave. Parents should not have to choose between the job they need and the family they love. We must immediately pass and sign into law the Family and Medical Leave Act. This bill will give American workers the right to take twelve weeks of unpaid leave per year in order to care for a newborn child or sick family member—a right enjoyed by workers in every other advanced industrial nation.

Child Support Enforcement. We will crack down on deadbeat parents by reporting them to credit agencies, so they can't borrow money for themselves when they're not taking care of their children. We'll use the Internal Revenue Service to collect child support, start a national deadbeat databank, and make it a felony to cross state lines to avoid paying support.

LIFETIME LEARNING

Putting people first demands a revolution in lifetime learning, a concerted effort to invest in the collective talents of our people. Education today is more than the key to climbing the ladder of opportunity. In today's global economy, it is an imperative for our nation. Our economic life is on the line.

Government fails when our schools fail. For four years we have heard much talk about "the Education President" but we have seen no government action to close the gap between what our people can achieve and what we ask of them. Washington shows little concern as people pay more and get less for what matters most to them: educating their children.

Millions of our children go to school unprepared to learn. The Republicans in Washington have promised—but never delivered—full funding of Head Start, a proven success that gives disadvantaged children a chance to get ahead. And while the states move forward with innovative ways to bring parents and children together, Washington fails to insist on responsibility from parents, teachers, students—and itself.

The 1980s witnessed the emergence of immense education gaps between America and the world, and among our own people. Test scores went down while violence in the schools went up. Too many children did bullet drills instead of fire drills, and too many teachers were assaulted. High school graduates who chose not to go to college saw their incomes drop by 20 percent. While college tuition and living costs skyrocketed, the Republicans tried to slash assistance for middle-class families. By the decade's end, nearly one of every two college students was dropping out, most because they simply could no longer afford it.

In an era when what you earn depends on what you learn, education too often stops at the schoolhouse door. While our global competitors invest in their working people, seven of every ten dollars American companies spend on employee training goes to those at the top of the corporate ladder. High-level executives float on golden parachutes to a cushy life while hardworking Americans are grounded without the skills they need.

Our national economic strategy for America will put people first at every stage of their lives. We will dramatically improve the way parents prepare their children for school, give students the chance to train for jobs or pay for college, and provide workers with the training and retraining they need to compete in tomorrow's economy.

The main elements include:

Parents and Children Together. We will inspire parents to take responsibility and empower them with the knowledge they need to help their children enter school ready to learn. As Arkansas does, we will help disadvantaged parents work with their children to build an ethic of learning at home that benefits both parent and child. We will fully fund programs that save us several dollars for every one we spend—Head Start; the Women, Infants and Children (WIC) program; and other critical initiatives recommended by the National Commission on Children.

Dramatically Improve K–12 Education. We will overhaul America's public schools to ensure that every child has a chance for a world-class education. We will establish tough standards and a national examination system in core subjects like math and science, level the playing field for disadvantaged students, and reduce class sizes. Every parent should have the right to choose the public school his or her child attends, as they do in Arkansas. In return, we will demand that parents work with their children to keep them in school, off drugs, and headed toward graduation.

Safe Schools Initiative. We will provide funds for violence-ridden schools to hire security personnel and purchase metal detectors, and we will help cities and states use community policing to put more police officers on the streets in high-crime areas where schools are located.

Youth Opportunity Corps. To give teenagers who drop out of school a second chance, we will help communities open youth centers. Teenagers will be matched with adults who care about them and given a chance to develop self-discipline and skills.

National Apprenticeship Program We will bring business, labor, and education leaders together to develop a national apprenticeship-style system that offers non-college-bound students training in valuable skills, with the promise of good jobs when they graduate.

National Service Trust Fund. To give every American the right to borrow money for college, we will retain the Pell grant program but scrap the existing student loan program and establish a National Service Trust Fund. Those who borrow from the fund will be able to choose how to repay the balance: either as a small percentage of their earnings over time, or by serving their communities doing work their country needs as teachers, law enforcement officers, health-care workers, or peer counselors helping kids stay off drugs and in school.

Worker Retraining. We will require every employer to spend 1.5 percent of payroll for continuing education and training, and make them provide the training to all workers, not just executives. Workers will be able to choose advanced skills training, the chance to earn a high school diploma, or the opportunity to learn to read. And we will streamline the confusing array of publicly funded training programs.

AFFORDABLE QUALITY HEALTH CARE

The American health-care system costs too much and does not work. Instead of putting people first, Washington favors the insurance companies, drug manufacturers, and health-care bureaucracies. We cannot build tomorrow's economy until we guarantee every American the right to affordable quality health care.

Washington has ignored the needs of middle-class families and let health-care costs soar out of control. American drug companies have raised their prices three times faster than the rate of inflation, forcing American consumers to pay up to six times more than Canadians or Europeans pay for the same drugs. Insurance companies routinely deny coverage to consumers with "pre-existing conditions" and waste billions on bureaucracy and administration. Twelve years ago, Americans spent $249 billion on health care. This year we'll spend more than $800 billion.

Health-care costs are now the number one cause of bankruptcy and labor disputes. They threaten our ability to compete, adding, for example, $700 to the cost of every car made in America. Our complex system chokes consumers and providers with paper, requiring the average doctor to spend eighty hours a month on paperwork. It invites fraud and abuse. We spend more on health care than any nation on earth and don't get our money's worth.

Our people still live in fear. Today almost 60 million Americans have inadequate health insurance—or none at all. Every year working men and women are forced to pay more while their employers cover less. Small businesses are caught between going broke and doing right by their employees. Infants die at rates that exceed countries blessed with far fewer resources. Across our nation older Americans live in fear that they will fall ill—and lose everything or bankrupt their children's dreams trying to pay for the care they deserve.

America has the potential to provide the world's best, most advanced and cost-effective health care. What we need are leaders who are willing to take on the insurance companies, the drug companies, and the health-care bureaucracies and bring health-care costs down.

Our health-care plan is simple in concept but revolutionary in scope. First, we will move to radically control costs by changing incentives, reducing paperwork, and cracking down on drug and insurance company practices. As costs drop, we will phase in guaranteed universal access to basic medical coverage through employer or public programs.

Companies will be required to insure their employees, with federal assistance in the early years to help them meet their obligations. Health-care providers will finally have incentives to reduce costs and improve quality for consumers. Savings from cost containment will help those who pay too much for health insurance today. American health care will make sense.

Our plan will put people first by guaranteeing quality, affordable health care. No American will go without health care, but in return everyone who can must share the cost of his or her care. The main elements include:

National Spending Caps. The cost of health care must not be allowed to rise faster than the average American's income. We will scrap the Health Care Financing Administration and replace it with a health standards board—made up of consumers, providers, business, labor, and government—that will establish annual health budget targets and outline a core benefits package.

Universal Coverage. Affordable quality health care will be a right, not a privilege. Under our plan, employers and employees will either purchase private insurance or opt to buy into a high-quality public program. Every American not covered by an employer will receive the core benefits package set by the health standards board.

Managed Care Networks. Consumers will have access to a variety of local health networks, made up of insurers, hospitals, clinics, and doctors. The networks will receive a fixed amount of money for each consumer, giving them the necessary incentive to control costs.

Eliminating Drug Price Gouging. To protect American consumers and bring down prescription drug prices, we will eliminate tax breaks for drug companies that raise their prices faster than Americans' incomes rise.

Taking on the Insurance Industry. To stand up to the powerful insurance lobby and stop consumers from paying billions in administrative waste, we need to streamline the industry. Our health plan will institute a single claim form and ban underwriting practices that waste billions to discover which patients are bad risks. Any insurance company that wants to do business will have to take all comers and charge every business in a community the same rate. No company will be able to deny coverage to individuals with pre-existing conditions.

Fighting Bureaucracy and Billing Fraud. To control costs and trim the "paper hospital," our plan will replace expensive and complex financial forms and accounting procedures with a simplified, streamlined billing system. All Americans will carry "smart cards" coded with their personal medical information. We will also crack down on billing fraud and remove incentives that invite abuse.

A Rational Medical Liability System. To reduce litigation costs and keep doctors from practicing "defensive medicine," we will help develop alternative dispute-resolution mechanisms in every state. These procedures will effectively and humanely resolve legal challenges.

Core Benefits Package. Every American will be guaranteed a basic health benefits package that includes ambulatory physician care, inpatient hospital care, prescription drugs, and basic mental health care. The package will allow consumers to choose where to receive care and will include expanded preventive treatments such as pre-natal care, mammograms, and routine health screenings. We'll provide more services to the elderly and the disabled by expanding Medicare to include more long-term care.

Equitable Costs. We will protect small businesses through "community rating," which requires insurers to spread risk evenly among all companies.

A REVOLUTION IN GOVERNMENT

We cannot put people first and create jobs and economic growth without a revolution in government. We must take away power from the entrenched bureaucracies and special interests that dominate Washington.

We can no longer afford to pay more for—and get less from—our government. The answer for every problem cannot always be another program or more money. It is time to radically change the way government operates— to shift from top-down bureaucracy to entrepreneurial government that empowers citizens and communities to change our country from the bottom up. We must reward the people and ideas that work and get rid of those that don't.

It's long past time to clean up Washington. The last twelve years were nothing less than an extended hunting season for high-priced lobbyists and Washington influence peddlers. On streets where statesmen once strolled, a never-ending stream of money now changes hands— tying the hands of those elected to lead.

Millions of hardworking Americans struggle to make ends meet while their government no longer fights for their values or their interests. Washington deregulated the savings-and-loan industry and then tried to hide when it collapsed, leaving taxpayers to foot the bill. Political action committees and other special interests funnel more than $2.5 million every week to Congress, giving incumbents a 12–1 financial advantage over challengers.

During the 1980s the White House staff routinely took taxpayers for a ride to play golf or bid on rare stamps. High-level executive branch employees traded in their government jobs for the chance to make millions lobbying their former bosses. Experts estimate that nearly one of every two senior American trade officials has signed on to work for nations they once faced across the negotiating table.

This betrayal of democracy must stop.

To break the stalemate in Washington, we have to attack the problem at its source: entrenched power and money. We must cut the bureaucracy, limit special interests, stop the revolving door, and cut off the unrestricted flow of campaign funds. The privilege of public service ought to be enough of a perk for people in government.

We will focus on the following areas:

Staff Reductions. We will reduce the White House staff by 25 percent and challenge Congress to do the same.

Elimination of 100,000 Unnecessary Positions in the Bureaucracy. We will cut 100,000 federal government positions through attrition.

Cuts in Administrative Waste. We will require federal managers and workers to achieve 3 percent across-the-board administrative savings in every federal agency.

Cuts in Wasteful Government Spending Programs. We will eliminate taxpayer subsidies for narrow special interests, reform defense procurement and foreign aid, and get rid of spending programs that no longer serve their purpose.

Line Item Veto. To eliminate pork-barrel projects and cut government waste, we will ask Congress to give the President the line item veto.

Special Interest Tax. To help put government back in the hands of the people, we will ask Congress to eliminate the tax deductions for special interest lobbying expenses. We will also urge Congress to close the "lawyers' loophole," which allows lawyer-lobbyists to disguise lobbying activities on behalf of foreign governments and powerful corporations.

Stopping the Revolving Door. We will require all top appointees to sign a pledge that, if they work in our Administration, they will refrain from lobbying government agencies within their responsibilities for five years after leaving office. We will require senior officials to pledge never to become registered agents on behalf of any foreign government. We will then challenge members of Congress to do the same.

Lobbyists. We will push for and sign legislation to toughen and streamline lobbying disclosure. The new law will require all special interest groups to register with the Office of Government Ethics within thirty days after contacting a federal official, lawmaker, or lawmaker's aide. Lobbyists will be required to report twice a year on their contacts and expenses. We will instruct the Justice Department to strictly enforce disclosure laws and collect fines.

Campaign Finance Reform. We will push for and sign strong campaign finance legislation to cap spending on House and Senate campaigns; cut political action committee (PAC) contributions in any race to the individual legal limit of $1000; lower the cost of airtime so that television becomes an instrument of education, not a weapon of political assassination; and require lobbyists who appear before Congressional committees to disclose the campaign contributions they've made to committee members.

The economic projections that follow demonstrate how our plan will close America's investment gap while cutting the budget deficit.

The plan not only pays for every penny in new investment with new savings, but—even with modest growth estimates—will cut the deficit in half by 1996. Combined with smart investments, these savings will help get spending under control and put our economy back on track.

INVESTMENTS AND SAVINGS
In billions of dollars

New Investments	1993	1994	1995	1996
Putting America to work	28.3	34.6	35.4	35.4
Rewarding work and families	3.5	5.5	6.5	7.0
Lifetime learning	10.1	14.25	17.27	21.7
Total	41.9	54.35	59.17	64.1
New Savings				
Spending cuts	26.09	32.42	36.81	44.98
Entitlement reform	0.6	1.0	1.0	1.8
Tax fairness	19.8	22.7	23.9	25.3
Closing corporate loopholes	11.3	14.4	15.3	17.3
Total	57.79	70.52	77.01	89.38

DEFICIT PROJECTIONS
In billions of dollars

	1993	1994	1995	1996
Current deficit*	323.0	268.0	212.0	193.0
Clinton-Gore plan: moderate growth	295.7	243.0	174.0	141.0
Clinton-Gore plan: strong growth	282.6	207.02	125.54	75.84

Based on Congressional Budget Office growth assumptions.

BREAKDOWN OF SAVINGS
In billions of dollars

Spending Cuts	1993	1994	1995	1996
Defense cuts (beyond Bush)	2.0	8.5	10.5	16.5
Intelligence cuts	1.0	1.5	1.5	1.5
Administrative savings	2.0	5.0	6.5	8.5
100,000 federal workers	2.0	4.3	4.5	4.5
Cut White House staff by 25 percent	0.01	0.01	0.01	0.01
Reform debt financing	0.0	2.0	2.0	2.0
Cut Congressional staff by 25 percent	0.1	0.1	0.1	0.1

BREAKDOWN OF SAVINGS (*CONT.*)
In billions of dollars

Spending Cuts	1993	1994	1995	1996
Line item veto to cut pork-barrel projects	3.8	2.0	2.0	2.0
Reform Defense Department procurement management	5.7	0.0	0.0	0.0
Reform Defense Department inventory system	2.3	2.5	2.5	2.5
Create comprehensive federal agency energy conservation program	0.0	0.85	0.85	0.85
Reduce overhead on federally sponsored university research	0.73	0.76	0.79	0.82
Streamline USDA field offices	0.035	0.075	0.13	0.14
Reduce special-purpose HUD grants	0.12	0.12	0.13	0.13
Index nuclear waste disposal fees for inflation	0.02	0.04	0.06	0.08

BREAKDOWN OF SAVINGS *(CONT.)*
In billions of dollars

Spending Cuts	1993	1994	1995	1996
RTC (Resolution Trust Corporation) management reform	4.0	4.0	4.5	4.6
End taxpayer subsidies for honey producers	0.02	0.02	0.0	0.0
Consolidate overseas broadcasting system	0.08	0.18	0.26	0.27
Freeze spending on federal consultants	0.17	0.19	0.21	0.21
Consolidate social service programs	0.0	0.27	0.27	0.27
Reform foreign aid pipeline	2.0	0.0	0.0	0.0
Subtotal	26.09	32.42	36.81	44.98

Entitlement Reform

	1993	1994	1995	1996
Increase Medicare-B costs for those with incomes of more than $125,000	0.6	1.0	1.0	1.8

Tax Fairness

Increase rates on top 2 percent, raise Alternative Minimum Tax, surtax on millionaires	17.8	20.5	21.6	23.0
Prevent tax fraud on unearned income for the wealthy	2.0	2.2	2.3	2.3
Subtotal	19.8	22.7	23.9	25.3

Closing Corporate Loopholes

Limit corporate deductions at $1 million for CEOs	0.1	0.4	0.4	0.4
End incentives for opening plants overseas	0.3	0.4	0.4	0.4
Prevent tax avoidance by foreign corporations	9.0	11.0	11.5	13.5
Increase fines and taxes for corporate polluters	1.8	2.5	2.9	2.9
Eliminate tax deduction for lobbying cxpcnscs	0.1	0.1	0.1	0.1
Subtotal	11.3	14.4	15.3	17.3
Total	57.79	70.52	77.01	89.38

While *Putting People First* is the heart of our plan to get our economy moving again, it is not all-inclusive. Many other crucial challenges await the next President and Vice President: healing the divisions that threaten our society, restoring law and order to our streets and communities, protecting a woman's right to choose, launching a war on AIDS, leading the world in protecting our environment, and securing America's interests and promoting democracy around the world.

In the pages that follow, we offer our plans and thoughts on these and other crucial issues. No reader will find an answer to every question of local, national, or international concern. But we hope that these outlines will give you a better sense of where we stand and what we can all do to change America.

Agriculture

IF THERE IS one thing that has united Americans through-out our history, it is the feeling we have for this rich and expansive land. Our forebears were passionate about it. Farmers and pioneers, they made these 2 billion acres we call America the canvas of their dreams.

We appreciate how much American farmers have done for their country. The commitment and sacrifice of those who feed not only the United States, but also much of the world, must not go unnoticed. A Clinton–Gore Administration will support an agriculture policy that both recognizes the small-family producers who have done so much to make America great and treats consumers and taxpayers fairly.

We understand that guaranteeing an adequate quality food supply is an important strategic goal of the United States. Our current farm programs, properly managed, can achieve reasonable prices for producers and guarantee a safe and stable food and fiber supply for consumers. We believe that American farmers are the most competitive and efficient in the world. And as President and Vice President, we will help them stay that way.

Here's what we'll do:

Trade

• Work hard to *open new markets for American agricultural products,* particularly in Eastern Europe and the Commonwealth of Independent States (the former Soviet Union).

• *Support full use of federal export tools like the Export Enhancement Program* (EEP) to expand trade and enter new markets.

• Act swiftly to *level the playing field in international trade* when foreign competitors use export subsidies to gain an unfair advantage over American farmers—instead of sitting idly by as the Bush Administration has done.

• *Remove unfair trade barriers* through tough negotiation with our trading partners to *pry open closed markets,* including the support of reciprocal retaliation against the European Community unless the E.C. removes its ban on U.S. pork.

Protecting Our Environment

• *Include farmers in the national debate on environmental policy.* Farmers and ranchers are among the best stewards of the land; they pay taxes and bank notes on their land and they ought to have a say in what is done with it.

• *Ensure that environmental decisions are based on sound scientific data,* not politics, and that America's farmers alone do not carry the costs of environmental protection.

Expand Food Aid

- *Expand food aid overseas* to assist emerging democracies and developing nations.
- *Increase funding for the Food for Peace program.*

Research, Development, and New Ideas

- Provide American leadership in world agriculture through *modernization and development of current farm programs* and expansion of agriculture research and development.
- *Bring existing farm programs into the communications age* by equipping federal agriculture offices with the most modern communications and computer equipment available.
- *Consolidate forms and processes* to cut down on wasted time and delays.
- *Utilize federal research funds* to improve cooperation among farmers and among states in the same region.

A Department for Agriculture

- *Give American farmers a friend and advocate* at the USDA by appointing a Secretary of Agriculture who is respected by American farmers and who will work tirelessly on their behalf. The USDA must be a department *for* agriculture, not an annex to the Office of Management and Budget or the State Department.

AIDS

FIGHTING the AIDS epidemic will be a top priority of a Clinton–Gore Administration. If we fail to commit our hearts and resources now to fighting AIDS, we will pay a far greater price in the future, both in deaths and in dollars. We need a President and Vice President who will focus national attention on AIDS, to encourage compassion and understanding, to promote education, and to speak out against intolerance.

We can't afford another four years without a plan to declare war on AIDS. We can't afford to have yet another President who remains silent about AIDS or who puts the issue on the back burner. It's time for change and real leadership.

In order to fight AIDS we will:

* Increase funding for desperately needed new initiatives in research, prevention, and treatment.
* Appoint an AIDS policy director to coordinate federal AIDS policies, cut through bureaucratic red tape, and implement recommendations made by the National Commission on AIDS.
* Speed up the drug approval process and commit increased resources to research and development of AIDS-related treatments and vaccines, ensuring that

women and people of color are included in research and drug trials.

• Fully fund the Ryan White Care Act. Work closely with individuals and communities that are affected by HIV to create a partnership between the federal government and those with knowledge and experience in fighting HIV.

• Promote a national AIDS education and prevention initiative that disseminates frank and accurate information to reduce the spread of the disease and educates our children about the nature and threat of AIDS.

• Provide quality health coverage to all Americans with HIV as part of a broader national health-care program; work vigorously to improve access to promising experimental therapies for people with life-threatening illnesses; and improve preventive and long-term care.

• Combat AIDS-related discrimination and oppose needless mandatory HIV testing in federal organizations such as the Peace Corps, the Job Corps, and the Foreign Service; stop the cynical politicization of immigration policies by directing the Justice Department to follow the Department of Health and Human Services' recommendation that HIV be removed from the immigration restrictions list; promote legislation based on sound scientific and public health principles—not on panic, politics, and prejudice.

Prevention and Education

• Launch a strong and effective AIDS education campaign.

• Reevaluate the AIDS prevention budget at the U.S.

Centers for Disease Control to ensure that education is a top priority.

• Ensure that increased funding for prevention and services goes directly to community-based organizations that are on the front line of the battle against the HIV virus.

• Promote AIDS education in American schools.

• Provide drug treatment on demand to stop the spread of HIV by intravenous drug users.

• Increase funding for behavior and social science research so that we can better understand the behaviors that put people at risk for HIV.

• Support local efforts to make condoms available in our schools.

Treatment and Care

• Provide health care for all Americans, including those with HIV, through coverage they obtain either on the job or through government-mandated programs, which will include:

— Comprehensive inpatient and outpatient services, including frequent diagnostic monitoring, early intervention therapies, and psychological care.

— Prescription drugs and improved access to experimental therapies. Because treatments are not accessible unless they are affordable, a Clinton–Gore Administration will support legislation that denies tax breaks to companies that raise the cost of drugs beyond Americans' ability to pay for them.

— Adequate options for long-term home and community-based care that minimize unnecessary and wasteful hospitalizations.

— Voluntary, confidential, or anonymous testing for AIDS and HIV and counseling for every American who wants it.

• Encourage the Centers for Disease Control to periodically review their definition of AIDS to ensure that symptoms and infections that occur among women, people of color, and drug users are included in the federal definition. Those who qualify under revised definitions should be promptly made eligible for all federal benefit programs for people with AIDS.

• Develop programs with the Department of Health and Human Services to ensure that America's health care professionals are kept fully and regularly informed about diagnosing and treating HIV. Have the National Institutes of Health (NIH) develop a formalized mechanism to make sure that state-of-the-art information is broadly and rapidly disseminated to health professionals and people with HIV disease.

Research and Drug Development

• Work vigorously to develop a vaccine against AIDS and to find therapies that will destroy HIV, repair the immune system, and prevent and treat AIDS-related infections.

• Increase funding for both AIDS-specific and general biomedical research.

• Expand clinical and community-based trials for treatments and vaccines, and raise the level of participation of underrepresented populations.

• Reorganize the NIH infrastructure to streamline AIDS research efforts and improve planning, efficiency, and communication.

• Promote a more rapid review by the NIH of research grant applications and a speedier distribution of funding for approved studies.

• Facilitate greater access to drugs and work to speed up the drug approval process. Ensure that the Food and Drug Administration (FDA) has the resources to assist in the efficient design of AIDS-related drug trials and to review their results rapidly. The FDA will also make possible greater access to promising experimental therapies without compromising patient safety.

Discrimination

• Fight all AIDS-related discrimination as well as discrimination based on race, gender, and sexual orientation.

• Fully implement the Americans with Disabilities Act and resist any efforts to weaken its provisions. The Department of Justice and the U.S. Commission on Civil Rights must make it a high priority to monitor the occurrence of AIDS-related discrimination and the enforcement of the ADA with respect to HIV-related complaints.

• Forbid health insurance companies from denying coverage to HIV-positive applicants. Prohibit all health plans from adopting discriminatory caps or exclusions that provide lower coverage for AIDS than for any other life-threatening illnesses. No American will be denied health coverage because he or she loses a job or has a pre-existing condition.

- Oppose mandatory testing in federal organizations such as the Peace Corps, the Job Corps, and the Foreign Service.
- Lift the current ban on travel and immigration to the United States by foreign nationals with HIV.

Arms Control

THE END of the Cold War leaves two great tasks for American arms-control policy: to halt the spread of nuclear, chemical, biological, and missile technologies to countries that do not have them; and to turn the legacy of the Cold War into an effective strategy for the post–Cold War era.

Here's what we should do:

Oppose Nuclear Proliferation

• Bolster the International Atomic Energy Agency's capacity to inspect suspect facilities through surprise inspections in member countries.

• Lead a strong international effort to impose sanctions against companies or countries that spread dangerous weapons.

• Demand that other nations tighten their export laws and strengthen enforcement of policies regarding nuclear weapons.

• Never again subsidize the nuclear ambitions of a Saddam Hussein.

• Ensure that agricultural and other non-military loans to foreign governments are used as intended.

• Strengthen safeguards to ensure that key nuclear

technology and equipment are kept out of dictators' grasp.

Pursue and Strengthen International Agreements

• Ratify the START Treaty and the follow-on agreement of June 1992.
• Lead the effort to achieve a Comprehensive Test Ban Treaty through a phased approach.
• Make nonproliferation one of the highest priorities of our intelligence agencies.
• Press more nations to sign and abide by the Missile Technology Control Regime.
• Conclude a chemical weapons convention banning the production, stockpiling, or use of chemical weapons.

Nuclear Weapons Plans for the Twenty-first Century

• Maintain a survivable and stable nuclear deterrent that is consistent with our needs in the post–Cold War era.
• Focus our research and development on the goal of a limited missile defense system within the strict framework of the ABM Treaty. Deployment of a massive space-based defense such as Brilliant Pebbles is not necessary.
• Support research on limited missile defense systems to protect the United States against new long-range missile threats.
• Conduct all such activities in strict compliance with the Anti-Ballistic Missile (ABM) Treaty.

Arts

WE BELIEVE that the arts should play an essential role in educating and enriching all Americans. We will help the arts become an integral part of education in every community, broadening the horizons of our children and preserving our valuable cultural heritage. A Clinton–Gore Administration will ensure access to the arts for all of our citizens.

As President and Vice President, we will defend freedom of speech and artistic expression by opposing censorship or "content restrictions" on grants made by the National Endowment for the Arts. We will continue federal funding for the arts and promote the full diversity of American culture, recognizing the importance of providing all Americans with access to the arts.

Campaign Finance Reform

AMERICAN POLITICS is being held hostage by big money interests. Members of Congress now collect more than $2.5 million in campaign funds every week, while political action committees, industry lobbies, and cliques of $100,000 donors buy access to Congress and the White House.

George Bush recently vetoed the 1992 Campaign Finance Reform Bill in order to protect the special interests that support him. Americans pay for his inaction in decreased environmental and worker safety regulations, increased health-care costs, and weakened consumer regulations.

We believe it's long past time to clean up Washington. As part of our plan to fight the cynicism that is gripping the American people, we will support and sign strong campaign finance reform legislation to bring down the cost of campaigning and encourage real competition.

We can't go four more years without a plan to take away power from the entrenched bureaucracies and special interests that dominate Washington.

We will:

• *Place voluntary spending caps* on House and Senate races, depending on a state's population. These caps will level the playing field and encourage challengers to enter the race.

- *Limit political action committee (PAC) contributions* to the $1000 legal limit for individuals.
- *Reduce the cost of television airtime* to promote real discussion and turn TV into an instrument of education, not a weapon of political assassination.
- *Eliminate tax deductions for special interest lobbying expenses* and the "lawyers' loophole," which allows lawyer-lobbyists to disguise lobbying activities on behalf of foreign governments and powerful corporations.
- *Require lobbyists* who appear before Congressional committees *to disclose the campaign contributions* they've made to members of those committees. The public has a right to know when moneyed interests are trying to influence elected officials in Washington.
- *End the unlimited "soft" money* contributions that are funneled through national, state, and local parties to presidential candidates.

Children

FOR FAR too long we have failed to address the needs of America's children. We do not provide them with adequate health care, the best education, or protection from violence, and we do not address the special problems of the disadvantaged. We need bold reform to help all our children reach their potential.

Children are America's future. As parents, we have long fought to make that future bright—for better education, improved child health care, and real drug prevention. With renewed vigor, we will carry that fight into the future.

Our children and our country cannot afford another four years of neglect from Washington. The next generation of young people should not be America's first to grow up with less hope than their parents. It's time to act to help our children.

Here's how:

Guarantee Affordable Quality Health Care

• Control costs, improve quality, and cover everybody under a *national health-care* plan. Our plan will require insurers to offer a core package of benefits, including pre-natal care and other important preventive care benefits.

• Create a nationwide program like Arkansas's *Good Beginnings* to provide *health-care services to more low-income women* and their children.

• Develop a *comprehensive maternal and child health network* to reduce both the infant mortality rate and the number of low-birth-weight babies—because every child deserves a fighting chance to grow up healthy.

• *Fully fund the Women, Infants and Children (WIC) program* and other critical initiatives recommended by the National Commission on Children that save us several dollars for every one we spend.

Revolutionize Lifetime Learning

• Make good on the Bush Administration's broken promises by *fully funding Head Start* and other pre-school programs.

• Through innovative parenting programs like the Home Instructional Program for Pre-school Youngsters (HIPPY), *help disadvantaged parents work with their children* to build an ethic of learning at home that benefits both parent and child.

• *Dramatically improve K–12 education* by establishing tough standards and a national examination system in core subjects, leveling the playing field for disadvantaged students, and reducing class sizes.

• Give every parent the right to *choose the public school his or her child attends,* as is the case in Arkansas.

• *Create a Youth Opportunity Corps* to give teenagers who drop out of school a second chance. Community youth centers will match teenagers with adults who care about them, and will give kids a chance to develop self-discipline and skills.

• *Develop a national apprenticeship-style system* to give kids who don't want to go to college the skills they need to find high-wage jobs.

• *Give every American the opportunity to borrow money for college:* retain the Pell grant program but scrap the existing college loan program and establish a National Service Trust Fund. Those who borrow from the fund will be able to repay the balance either as a small percentage of their earnings over time, or through community service—as teachers, law enforcement officers, health-care workers, or peer counselors helping kids stay off drugs and in school.

Make Our Homes, Schools, and Streets Safer for Children

• Crack down on violence against women and children. Sign the *Violence Against Women Act,* which would provide tougher enforcement and stiffer penalties to deter domestic violence.

• Launch a *Safe Schools Initiative* so kids can focus on learning again: make schools eligible for federal assistance to pay for metal detectors and security personnel if they need them; encourage states to grant school officials greater authority to conduct locker and automobile searches; and fund mentoring and outreach programs so kids in trouble with crime, drugs, or gangs will have someone to turn to.

• Establish *school-based clinics and drug education*

programs to prevent drug abuse and to help kids who get hooked on drugs. Promote AIDS education in our schools.

• *Set standards for crime emergency areas* by making communities hit hardest by crime eligible for federal matching funds to assist in the war on crime when they adopt proven anti-crime measures.

• Fight crime by putting *100,000 new police officers* on the streets; create a National Police Corps and offer unemployed veterans and active military personnel a chance to become law enforcement officers here at home.

• *Expand community policing,* fund more drug treatment, and establish community "boot camps" to discipline first-time nonviolent offenders.

• Sign the Brady Bill, which will *create a waiting period for the purchase of handguns* and allow authorities to conduct background checks before guns fall into the wrong hands.

• *Work to ban assault rifles,* which have no legitimate hunting purpose.

Support Pro-family and Pro-children Policies

• *Expand the Earned Income Tax Credit* to guarantee a "working wage," so that no American who works full-time is forced to raise children in poverty.

• Lower the tax burden on middle-class Americans by asking the very wealthy to pay their fair share; give middle-class taxpayers a *choice between a children's tax credit or a significant reduction in their income tax rate.* Virtually every industrialized nation recognizes the importance of strong families in its tax code; we should, too.

• *Sign into law the Family and Medical Leave Act,* which George Bush vetoed in 1990, so that no worker is forced to choose between maintaining his or her job and caring for a newborn child or sick family member.

• Create a *child-care network* as complete as the public school network, tailored to the needs of working families; establish more *rigorous standards for licensing child-care facilities* and implement improved methods for enforcing them.

• Promote *tough child support legislation* and develop stricter, more effective methods to enforce it: crack down on deadbeat parents by reporting them to credit agencies, so they can't borrow money for themselves when they're not taking care of their children; use the Internal Revenue Service to collect child support; start a national deadbeat databank; and make it a felony to cross state lines to avoid paying support.

Cities

WHILE AMERICA'S great cities fall into disrepair, Washington continues to ignore their fate. Private enterprise has abandoned our cities, leaving our young people with few job prospects and declining hopes. Our nation cannot move forward until our cities become centers of expanding opportunity and engines of economic growth. Prosperous cities are the key to vital regional economies and to safe and healthy suburbs.

We believe it is time for a new partnership to rebuild America's cities—a partnership between people and their government to expand opportunity and solve problems, so that our cities will once again be the pride of our nation. America's cities should be places where hardworking families can put down roots and find good jobs, affordable housing, decent schools, and safe streets. Hope and opportunity—not mean streets and drug pushers—must prevail.

To rebuild America's cities, the most important thing we can do is to implement a national economic strategy that pulls us out of the recession and gets our country moving again. An expanding economy is the best way to revitalize our cities.

For the past twelve years, Republican administrations have told us that we can turn our backs on our cities and still thrive as a nation. They've encouraged us to think that our cities' problems are not America's problems, that we have no responsibility to help city dwellers improve their lives. We believe they are wrong.

President Bush is right to speak out against the violence that stalks our children. But he is wrong to cut back on funds that cities use to hire more police officers for the street—and to oppose the Brady Bill, which even Ronald Reagan supports.

Whether we live in cities or suburbs or quiet rural hamlets, all Americans are paying for the unraveling of the American community. We are paying for the denial and the neglect of the last decade and more. We have the highest crime rate of any advanced nation in the world, and every year more of our tax dollars go for jails instead of for schools and jobs.

The 1980s saw the concrete foundations of the United States crumble as the investment gap widened between America and our global competitors. By the decade's end, Japan and Germany were investing more than twelve times what we spend on roads, bridges, sewers, and the information networks and the technologies of the future. No wonder they threaten to surpass America in manufacturing by 1996. No wonder we are slipping behind. America's cities need help.

Here's what we'll do to get them back on track:

THREE PRINCIPLES

Opportunity: We can't rebuild our urban communities with handouts alone—we need a massive expansion of opportunity. The federal government should create conditions conducive to economic recovery through a national economic strategy, targeted incentives and grants designed to revitalize the urban economy, and measures that empower city residents to take advantage of newly created opportunities through expanded education, job training, and child-care services. In return for federal assistance, the cities will adopt comprehensive strategies leading to revitalized urban centers; take advantage of opportunities created by the federal/municipal partnership to attract business and expand the urban economic base; and play a key role in the empowerment of urban residents as the primary provider of education, housing, and crime prevention.

Community: Community groups and local citizen organizations will be the backbone of our urban improvement efforts. To restore our cities, we must create a new partnership committed to excellence and community service. The federal government must get involved again, working together with state and local authorities in this endeavor. Nonprofit organizations also have a role to play.

Responsibility: We must recognize that no matter how hard we work to make the federal/municipal partnership a success, we will make no progress unless individuals take responsibility for their own lives, working tirelessly to overcome challenges and solve problems in their families and communities.

Investing in Communities

• *Target funding and Community Development Block Grants* to rebuild America's urban roads, bridges, water and sewage-treatment plants and low-income housing stock, stressing "ready to go" projects. Require companies that bid on these projects to set up a portion of their operations in low-income neighborhoods and employ local residents.

• Create a *nationwide network of community development banks* to provide small loans to low-income entrepreneurs and homeowners in the inner cities. These banks will provide advice and assistance to entrepreneurs, invest in affordable housing, and help mobilize private lenders.

• Create *urban enterprise zones* in stagnant inner cities, but only for companies willing to take responsibility by hiring inner city residents. Business taxes and federal regulations will be minimized to provide incentives to set up shop. In return, companies will have to make jobs for local residents a top priority.

• Ease the credit crunch in our inner cities, by passing a *more progressive Community Reinvestment Act* to prevent redlining and require financial institutions to invest in their communities.

• Create a *City Assistance Flexibility Program* to allow cities to redirect the use of 15 percent of the federal assistance they receive to meet their own community priorities and fund their local revitalization strategies.

Empowerment Through Economic Opportunity

• *Expand and improve job training* by requiring every employer to spend 1.5 percent of payroll for continuing education and training, and make them provide the training to all workers, not just executives.

• To ensure that no one with a family who works full-time has to raise children in poverty, we will *increase the Earned Income Tax Credit* to make up the difference between a family's earnings and the poverty level.

• *Scrap the current welfare system* to make welfare a second chance, not a way of life. We will empower people on welfare with the education, training, and child care they need for up to two years so they can break the cycle of dependency. After that, those who are able will be required to work, either in the private sector or through community service.

• Require that any corporation receiving a multimillion-dollar federal contract create a *mentorship, after-school employment, or summer employment program for urban and rural disadvantaged youth.* This will expand horizons and create incentives for kids to stay in school.

A National Crime Strategy

• Fight crime by putting *100,000 new police officers* on the streets of America. We will create a National Police Corps and offer unemployed veterans and active military personnel a chance to become law enforcement officers here at home.

• *Set standards for crime emergency areas.* Hard-hit communities will be eligible for federal matching funds to assist in the war on crime, if they create a comprehensive crime control plan that measures results and adopts proven anti-crime measures, such as community-based policing to put more police on the beat, and "boot camps" for first-time nonviolent offenders.

• Pass the *Brady Bill,* which creates a waiting period for handgun purchases, to keep firearms out of the hands of criminals; *ban assault rifles,* like the so-called Street Sweeper, which have no legitimate hunting purpose; *limit access to multiple round clips* like the one used in the tragic killings in Killeen, Texas.

• Give public housing residents the opportunity to organize themselves to eliminate drugs and weapons from public housing projects and support efforts like *Operation Clean Sweep in Chicago,* which helps residents take their housing back from gangs and dealers.

• Provide funds for a *Safe Schools Initiative* to help violence-ridden schools hire security personnel and purchase metal detectors; help cities and states use community policing to put more police officers on the streets in high-crime areas where schools are located.

Rebuilding Our Urban Infrastructure

• Target funding and Community Development Block Grants to *rebuild America's urban roads, bridges, water and sewage-treatment plants, and low-income housing stock,* stressing "ready to go" projects. Require companies that bid on these projects to set up a portion of their operations in low-income neighborhoods and employ local residents.

• Allocate greater resources to *"intelligent vehicle"*

and roadway technology to reduce traffic and make more efficient use of current transportation resources.

• Increase the decision-making role of municipalities and community development groups so they can allocate a greater share of their transportation funds for *mass transit systems;* require cities to undertake more comprehensive planning before allocating funds, to guarantee that transportation dollars are actually spent meeting the goals of their revitalization plans and prevent money from being used for conflicting purposes.

• Ensure that federal matching fund rates provide incentives for programs that *repair existing facilities and increase efficiency,* instead of simply building more and more roads.

New Hope for Affordable Housing

• *Increase the ceiling on Federal Housing Authority (FHA) mortgage insurance* to 95 percent of the price of a home in an average metropolitan area, to make it easier for half a million American families to buy their first home.

• Make home ownership possible for lower-income Americans through *federal support of low-income, long-term housing buy-out programs* like Tampa's innovative Resurrection of Affordable Housing Program, in which condemned houses are purchased, restored, and sold to low-income buyers through a package of long-term subsidized financing.

• Require the Department of Housing and Urban Development (HUD) and the Department of Justice to *ag-*

gressively enforce existing civil rights laws to open up housing currently closed by discrimination.

• *Maintain the mortgage revenue bond program* to make affordable housing a reality.

• *Continue and strengthen the HOME Program,* by giving more authority to local administrative officials. Congress created the HOME program in 1990 to provide additional decent rental housing for low-income Americans, but limited localities' choices in utilizing HOME funds for new construction at the Bush Administration's urging.

• *Permanently extend the Low Income Housing Tax Credit.* This innovative provision helps attract private investment in housing for low-income renters and develops housing that would otherwise not be built. More than 120,000 homes a year are produced with the credit's help.

• Preserve our nation's enormous investment of billions of dollars in public housing since the Second World War by *ensuring that adequate funding for maintenance and upkeep is included in the HUD budget.*

Fighting Homelessness

• *Transfer 10 percent of HUD and other government-controlled housing* to community nonprofit organizations and churches to house the homeless.

• *Use housing available at closed military bases for homeless people,* with a preference for homeless veterans.

• *Develop targeted strategies to help different homeless populations*—those who need supported living environments, those who need residential alcohol and drug treatment, and those who simply can't afford to house their families.

• Hold a *Housing and Homelessness Summit* with urban leaders and mayors to create a new consensus for poverty programs, funding levels, and federal assistance for innovative housing crisis solutions.

Empowerment Through Education

• Fully fund *Head Start,* to ensure that our children arrive in school ready to learn, and the *Women, Infants and Children (WIC) program,* as well as other critical initiatives recommended by the National Commission on Children. These programs are proven successes that save us several dollars for every one we spend.

• Expand innovative parenting programs like Arkansas's Home Instructional Program for Pre-school Youngsters, which helps disadvantaged parents work with their children to *build an ethic of learning at home* that benefits both.

• *Increase Chapter One funding* to allow schools greater spending flexibility so they can reduce class sizes and make other local improvements.

• Give teenagers who drop out of school a second chance through a *Youth Opportunity Corps;* help communities open youth centers where teenagers are matched with adults who care about them and given the opportunity to develop self-discipline and skills.

• Dramatically improve K–12 education by establishing *tough national standards and a national examination system in core subjects* like math and science, leveling the playing field for disadvantaged students, and reducing class sizes.

- Provide every parent with the *right to choose the public school* his or her child attends, as they do in Arkansas; in return, demand that parents work with their children to keep them in school, off drugs, and headed toward graduation.

- *Expand health services and health-education programs in schools* to provide primary and preventive services and to fight teen pregnancy and AIDS.

- Bring business, education, and labor leaders together to develop a *national apprenticeship-style system* that offers non-college-bound students valuable skills training, with the promise of good jobs when they graduate.

- Give every American the right to borrow money for college by maintaining the Pell grant program, scrapping the existing student loan program, and *establishing a National Service Trust Fund.* Those who borrow from the fund will be able to choose how to repay the balance— either as a small percentage of their earnings over time or by returning to serve their communities as teachers, law enforcement officers, health-care workers, or peer counselors helping kids stay off drugs and in school.

- Give every adult American a chance to learn, to read and write, and to get a high school diploma with *adult literacy initiatives.*

Affordable Quality Health Care

- Establish a *national health care plan* that controls exploding health-care costs to guarantee every American, including the working poor who currently do not receive health insurance through their employers, affordable quality health care.

• Enact reforms, like *controlling drug costs and establishing health networks,* to decrease the strain on municipal health resources associated with the AIDS crisis and cut the enormous health-care costs of our city governments.

• *Improve health-care access in urban areas* through school- and community-based clinics to provide improved preventive care.

Civil Rights

FOR TWELVE YEARS Republicans have divided us against each other—pitting rich against poor, black against white, woman against man. They have fostered an atmosphere of blame and denial, instead of building an ethic of responsibility. President Bush and Vice President Quayle had the chance to bring out the best in us. Instead they appealed to our worst instincts.

A Clinton–Gore Administration will actively work to protect the civil rights of all Americans. Our Justice Department will aggressively prosecute offenders of civil rights laws and argue before the Supreme Court for interpretations of the Constitution that support its underlying content. And we will nominate jurists to the federal courts who have demonstrated wisdom, maturity, and intelligence in their legal work—jurists with a firm grounding in the rule of law and a firm belief in the fundamental importance of equal opportunity.

Because community depends on hope for a better future, a Clinton–Gore Administration will also work to empower all Americans economically. We will reverse the legacy of the Republicans and re-create that hope.

For too long we've been told about "us" and "them." Each and every election we see a new slate of arguments and ads telling us that "they" are the problem, not "us."

But there can be no "them" in America. There's only us. It's time to heal our scars, to make every American part of a nation that is coming together. Let us be bold and chart a new course.

Here's how we can help heal America:

Protect Rights for All

• *Support strong and effective enforcement of the 1991 Civil Rights Act* to ensure workplace fairness rules for all Americans. We have criticized President Bush for cynically characterizing the landmark 1991 Civil Rights Act as a quota bill.

• *Oppose racial quotas.*

• Strongly enforce the *Americans with Disabilities Act.*

• *Prohibit discrimination* in federal employment, federal contracts, and government services; issue executive orders to repeal the ban on gays and lesbians from military or foreign service.

• Support federal *civil rights legislation for gays and lesbians* that respects freedom of religion by exempting religious organizations, and that provides clear evidence standards to be used in court.

• Direct the Justice Department *to aggressively prosecute hate crimes* perpetrated against individuals because of their race, creed, religion, or sexual orientation.

• *Crack down on violence against women*—in the workplace, on college campuses, and in their homes; sign the Violence Against Women Act to provide tougher enforcement and stiffer penalities to deter domestic violence.

• Support the *Equal Remedies Act*, which lifts damages caps for women, people with disabilities, and religious minorities in workplace discrimination cases.

• Enforce Title IX, which *prohibits sex discrimination in education.*

• Sign the *Motor Voter Bill*, which President Bush vetoed, which would ease voter registration requirements and bring more Americans into the political process.

• Extend language assistance provisions in the *Voting Rights Act* to ensure language-minority Americans an equal opportunity to participate in the political process.

• *Support sovereignty and self-determination* of Native American tribal governments and promote true consultation and increased tribal authority in the administration of federal funds.

• Direct the Department of Interior to ensure that prior treaties and trust obligations are respected and fulfilled; and *protect tribal religious and spiritual freedoms,* including protection of sacred sites.

• Support *statehood for the District of Columbia.*

Economic Empowerment

• Fight for civil rights, not just by protecting individual liberties, but by providing *equal economic opportunity;* support new anti-poverty initiatives that move beyond the outdated answers of both major parties and instead reflect the values most Americans share: work, family, individual responsibility, community. Empower people to make their own choices and regain control of their destinies.

• Require every employer to spend 1.5 percent of payroll for *continuing education and job training*—and make them provide the training to all workers, not just executives. Workers will be able to choose advanced skills training, the chance to earn a high school diploma, or the opportunity to learn to read.

• *Expand the Earned Income Tax Credit,* by making up the difference between a family's earnings and the poverty level, to ensure that no one with a family who works full-time has to raise children in poverty.

• Bring business, labor, and education leaders together to develop a *national apprenticeship-style system* that offers non-college-bound students valuable skills training, with the promise of good jobs when they graduate.

• Launch a national network of *community development banks* to spur economic growth in urban and rural areas by making loans to low-income entrepreneurs who start new businesses and to homeowners.

Corporate Responsibility

OUR NATIONAL economic strategy will reward the people who work hard and play by the rules—the people who create new jobs, start new businesses, and invest in our people and our plants here at home. It will restore economic growth by helping free enterprise flourish and putting our people back to work.

We are going to do everything we can to make it easier for companies to compete in the world, with a better-trained workforce, cooperation between labor and management, fair and strong trade policies, and incentives to invest in America's economic growth. But we want the jet-setters of corporate America to know that if they sell their companies, their workers, and their country down the river, they'll get called on the carpet.

We can never again allow the corrupt do-nothing values of the 1980s to mislead us. Today, the average CEO at a major American corporation is paid 100 times more than the average worker. Our government rewards that excess with a tax break for executive pay, no matter how high it is, no matter what performance it reflects. And then the government hands out tax deductions to corporations that shut down their plants here and ship our jobs overseas. That has to change.

Never again can we allow Washington to reward those

who speculate in paper, instead of those who put people first. Never again can we sit idly by while the plight of hardworking Americans is ignored.

It's time to do right by the people who make America work.

Here's how:

Linking Pay and Performance

• Eliminate *tax deductions for excessive executive pay.*

• Encourage firms to reward workers for their performance and share profits with all employees by restricting companies' ability to *deduct special payments if they are limited to top executives.* Companies will be allowed to deduct bonuses tied to profits for top executives only if other employees also receive bonuses.

• Restore the link between pay and performance by encouraging companies to provide for *employee ownership and profit-sharing for all employees,* not just executives.

• Allow companies to deduct "golden parachute" payments to managers only if they *also provide severance packages for other employees.*

• *Permit shareholders to determine the compensation of top executives,* and require public corporations to provide understandable information on executive compensation to their stockholders.

Investing in America for a Change

• Eliminate tax breaks for American companies that shut down their American plants and *ship our jobs overseas.*

• Crack down on foreign companies in America that *prosper by manipulating our tax laws to their advantage.*

• Provide a *targeted investment tax credit* to encourage investment in the new plants and productive equipment here at home that we need to compete in the global economy.

• Help small businesses and entrepreneurs by offering a 50 percent tax exclusion to those who take risks by making *long-term investments in new businesses.*

• Make permanent the *research and development tax credit* to reward companies that invest in groundbreaking technologies.

Making Polluters Pay

• *Get tough on environmental crime* by holding companies and polluters responsible for their behavior. When corporations deliberately violate environmental laws, they'll pay the price—and, if necessary, polluters will go to jail.

• Create incentives for corporations to *curb industrial and toxic emissions* and reward those who control pollutants and recycle.

Reorganizing the Workplace

• Encourage greater *cooperation between labor and management;* set an example in the federal government by eliminating unnecessary layers of bureaucracy and putting more decision-making authority in the hands of front-line workers.

• Sign into law the *Family and Medical Leave Act,*

which would give American workers the right to take twelve weeks of unpaid leave in order to care for newborn children or sick family members—a right enjoyed by workers in every other advanced industrial nation.

• Require all employers to spend 1.5 percent of payroll for *continuing education and training,* and make them provide that training to all workers, not just executives.

• Create a *national health-care plan* to ensure that all businesses can and will provide health coverage for their employees.

Crime and Drugs

Despite all the tough talk we hear from Washington, crime and drug use are expanding dramatically in America. Today more people are victims of violent crime and more addicted to drugs than ever before. We have a national problem on our hands that requires a tough national response. The Clinton–Gore national crime strategy will use the powers of the White House to prevent and punish crime.

We need to put more police on the streets and more criminals behind bars. We need to help cities that fight crime in sensible ways—with community policing, drug treatment, and drug education. And we need an effective, coordinated drug interdiction program that stops the endless flow of drugs entering our schools, our streets, and our communities. A Clinton–Gore Administration will provide cities and states with the help they need.

America cannot permit another generation of Americans to grow up on streets too unsafe to walk. We have a plan to fight crime.

Here's what we'll do:

Make Neighborhoods Safe Again

• Fight crime by *putting 100,000 new police officers on the streets;* create a National Police Corps and offer veterans and active military personnel a chance to become law enforcement officers.

• Give young offenders a second opportunity to become decent citizens by supporting the creation of *"boot camps"* for nonviolent first-time offenders. These shock incarceration programs require rigorous exercise and arduous work to instill discipline, boost self-esteem, and teach decency and respect for the law.

Expand Federal Crime Assistance

• Set standards for urban, suburban, and rural crime emergency areas. Make communities hit hardest by crime eligible for federal matching funds to assist in the war on crime when they create a comprehensive crime control plan that gets results and adopts proven anti-crime measures like:

• *Community-based policing:* In communities across America, local law enforcement officials are stopping crimes before they happen by moving from emergency response to community-based law enforcement. By taking officers out of patrol cars and putting increasing numbers back on the beat, cities are winning the war on crime.

• *Drug treatment on demand:* Thousands of addicts have volunteered to take themselves off the streets, only to hear the government tell them that they have to wait six months. In a Clinton–Gore Administration, federal assistance will help communities dramatically increase their ability to offer drug treatment to everyone who needs help.

- *Drug education in schools:* With only 5 percent of the world's population, Americans consume approximately 50 percent of all illegal drugs. To decrease demand, we need to reach our kids when they are young and teach them the evils of drug abuse. Drug education programs and school-based clinics must provide our children with access to the drug counseling, education, and outreach programs they need to stop drug addiction before it begins.

Keep Guns Out of the Hands of Criminals

- Provide the leadership we need to *pass the Brady Bill,* which will create a waiting period for handgun purchases to keep firearms off the streets and out of the hands of criminals.
- *Ban assault weapons, like the so-called Street Sweeper, which have no legitimate hunting purpose;* limit access to multiple-round clips like the one used in the tragic killings in Killeen, Texas.

Empower Public Housing Residents

- Give residents of public housing the chance to organize themselves to eliminate the drugs and weapons from public housing; support efforts like *Operation Clean Sweep* in Chicago, which helps residents take back their housing from gangs and dealers.

Take Back Our Schools

• Create a *Safe Schools Initiative,* so that children can focus on learning again. We will increase funding to pay for metal detectors and security personnel; encourage states to grant school officials greater authority to conduct locker and automobile searches; and expand funding for mentoring, counseling, and outreach programs so kids in trouble with crime, gangs, or drugs can turn to someone for help.

Get Tough on White-Collar Crime

• We will work to pass *tougher criminal penalties* for white-collar crimes—including environmental crimes—so that serious white-collar criminals serve jail time.
• *Plea bargaining will be limited to questions of prison time,* not how much money a white-collar crook gets to keep.
• *Jail sentences will be served in real prisons,* not high-tech summer camps.

Defense Conversion

At the end of the Second World War, more than 75 million Americans lost their jobs, but our nation made the most of their skills and launched the greatest economic boom the world has ever seen. Now that the Cold War has been won, we cannot leave those who won that victory out in the cold.

Today we have a historic opportunity. The human and physical resources we once dedicated to winning the Cold War can now be rededicated to fulfilling unmet domestic needs. We can put the scientists, engineers, factory workers, and technicians now being displaced by defense cuts back to work in similar jobs. But to do that, we need to create a partnership among government, business, labor, and education—just as our competitors do.

Many of the skills and technologies required to rebuild America are similar to those now used in our defense industries. Under our national economic strategy, we will encourage companies that bid on projects to rebuild America to contract work to, or purchase, existing defense facilities; and we will order the Pentagon to conduct a national defense-jobs inventory to assist displaced workers; we shall also provide special conversion loans and grants to small business defense contractors. Small businesses create most of the new jobs in our economy, and they will be critical in providing new, high-tech jobs for former defense industry workers.

As we cut our defense budget, we must transfer the savings, dollar for dollar, into investment in the American economy—into roads, bridges, and highways, into advanced communications networks, into research, into schools.

We can lead this country out of recession and get our economy moving again. We will provide new incentives for business to create jobs and improve American competitiveness, make a major investment in our children's education and our workers' retraining, and renew our commitment to America's working families.

Here's what we'll do:

Put People First

• Offer early retirement and a prorated pension for military personnel with fifteen to twenty years of service to encourage *voluntary downsizing.*

• *Encourage states to offer incentives* like alternative certification programs for military personnel who retire to take jobs in critical professions like education, health, or law enforcement. Military retirement credits should be increased by one year for each year of such employment.

• Put 100,000 new police officers on the streets by *creating a National Police Corps* that offers veterans and active military personnel a chance to become law enforcement officers here at home.

• *Train military personnel for critical civilian professions* through an expansion of the Montgomery GI Bill: the new program would enable them to take a one-year educational leave of absence with pay before officially beginning their retirement.

• Create an education fund administered by the National Science Foundation to *provide grants for professionals formerly engaged in defense work* to master the latest developments in critical civilian technology fields such as biotechnology, synthetic materials, renewable energy resources, and environmental cleanup.

Target Defense Cuts to Infrastructure Investments

• *Transportation:* renovate our country's roads, bridges, and railroads; create more American jobs by developing a high-speed rail network to link our major cities and commercial hubs; invest in "smart" highway technology to expand the capacity, speed, and efficiency of our major roadways; and develop high-tech short-haul aircraft.

• *Create a national information network* to link every home, business, lab, classroom, and library by the year 2015; put public records, databases, libraries, and educational materials on line for public use to expand access to all kinds of information.

• Expand federal efforts to *develop environmental technology* and create the world's most advanced systems to recycle, treat toxic waste, modernize city sewage systems, and clean our air and water; and develop new, clean energy sources.

Conduct a National Defense-Jobs Inventory

• Redeploy the people, skills, and technologies which made our defense industry second to none during the Cold War to the commercial infrastructure industries we'll need to compete in a global economy. A national defense-jobs inventory will match current skills and facilities capabilities with those required for these different projects.

Emphasize Civilian Technology

• *Increase investment in civilian high-tech applied R&D and manufacturing technologies* as the need for military R&D diminishes, in order to create millions of high-wage jobs and smooth our transition from a defense-based to a commercial economy.

• *Reinvest every dollar* that would otherwise be cut from defense R&D and technology industries into federal civilian R&D and generic technology programs.

• *Create a civilian advanced technology agency* modeled after the successful Defense Advanced Research Projects Agency (DARPA), the Department of Defense's research and development arm. The new agency would sponsor civilian R&D and technology projects, create new jobs for scientists, technicians, and engineers, and develop and produce manufacturing expertise for state-of-the-art technologies and innovative new products.

• *Enact a permanent extension of the R&D tax credit* to stimulate private investment in civilian R&D.

Aid Small Businesses

• Make *special conversion loans and grants* available to small business defense contractors through the Small Business Administration (SBA).

• *Increase funding for the Export-Import Bank,* targeted to assist small businesses in developing export markets.

• Create a *small business Technical Extension Service* through the SBA, based on the successful Agriculture Extension and Minnesota's proven Project Outreach Program, to give small businesses easy access to technical expertise.

• Offer a *50 percent tax exclusion to small businesses and entrepreneurs who take risks* by making long-term investments in new ventures.

• Provide a *targeted investment tax credit* to encourage investment in new plants and productive equipment here at home so that we can convert innovative ideas into new products and compete in the global economy.

Assist Hard-Hit Communities

• Develop new regulations to *enable portions of bases which have been cleaned up environmentally to be transferred to commercial functions* prior to the cleanup of the entire base, as long as the transfer is consistent with public safety.

• *Facilitate the transfer of military land to surrounding communities* by selling facilities at slightly lower than market rates, as long as the purchaser has demonstrated that the intended long-term use will provide significant employment opportunities to the community that would not otherwise exist should the sale not go through. Purchasers buying land through this program who do not carry through with their intended plan will face financial penalties.

Finance Conversion

Every dollar we save by downsizing our armed forces and defense industries will be reinvested during our transition to a post–Cold War economy. Under our national economic strategy, we will pay for these and other investments and reduce the national deficit by cutting spending, closing corporate tax loopholes, and requiring the very wealthy to pay their fair share of taxes.

Americans with Disabilities

WE HAVE LONG recognized that people with disabilities are some of our nation's greatest untapped resources. We believe that all persons with disabilities must be fully integrated into mainstream American society, so they can live fulfilling and rewarding lives. During our years in public office, we have compiled strong records of supporting public and private initiatives to enhance the independence and productivity of persons with disabilities.

As President and Vice President, we will continue our efforts. We will actively involve people with disabilities in developing a national policy that promotes equality, opportunity, and community for all Americans.

A Clinton–Gore Administration will ensure that children with disabilities receive a first-rate education that suits their needs. People with disabilities will be able to live in their own homes, in their own communities. Adults with disabilities will work alongside their peers without disabilities. And people with disabilities will have access to comprehensive health-care and consumer-driven personal assistance services.

We must not rest until America has a national disability policy based on three simple creeds: inclusion, not exclusion; independence, not dependence; and empowerment, not paternalism.

Here's what we will do:

Americans with Disabilities Act

• Work to ensure that the *Americans with Disabilities Act* (ADA) is fully implemented and aggressively enforced—to empower people with disabilities to make their own choices and to create a framework for independence and self-determination. The ADA is not about handouts and it is not a giveaway—it guarantees the civil rights of American citizens with disabilities.

Health Care for All Americans

• *Provide all Americans with affordable, quality health coverage,* either through their workplaces or through a government program; prohibit insurance companies from denying coverage based on pre-existing conditions; and contain costs by taking on the insurance industry and the drug industries.

• *Expand long-term care choices* for Americans with disabilities.

Improve Educational Opportunities for Children with Disabilities

• Work to *ensure children with disabilities a first-rate education,* tailored to their unique needs but provided alongside their classmates without disabilities.

• Support increased funding for special education services and work to improve the enforcement of laws which *guarantee children with disabilities the right to a high-quality public education.*

• Support increased efforts to *integrate children with disabilities into their schools' regular activities,* instead of sectioning them off in special programs where they cannot interact with other students.

• *Expand early intervention programs in health care and education*—such as Head Start—to ensure that children with disabilities live full and productive lives.

Expand Employment Opportunities for Americans with Disabilities

• *Increase the amount of special education, professional training, and job training* to reduce the extraordinarily high unemployment rate among Americans with disabilities as part of national adult education, job training, and apprenticeship programs.

• *Sign into law the Family and Medical Leave Act,* which George Bush vetoed in 1990, so that no worker is forced to choose between keeping his or her job and caring for a newborn child or sick family member.

Education

GOVERNMENT FAILS when our schools fail. For four years we've heard a lot of talk about "the Education President" but seen little government action to invest in the collective talents of our people. America needs leaders who show up for class every day, not just once every four years. In the first 100 days of a Clinton–Gore Administration, we'll give Congress and the American people a real education reform package. We'll work day and night to get it passed—unlike our current President, who often proposes legislation and then forgets about it.

Millions of our children go to school unprepared to learn. The Republicans in Washington have promised— but never delivered—full funding for Head Start, a proven success that gives disadvantaged children the opportunity to get ahead. And while states move forward with innovative ideas to bring parents and children together, Washington fails to insist on responsibility from parents, teachers, students—and itself.

We have to work hard to see that every American school has a challenging, rich curriculum, and that every teacher has the opportunity to develop the skills that he or she needs to teach well. Too often our schools move people up the ladder whether they study or not, graduate people whether they know anything or not, and dump people in the workforce whether they have real skills or not. And that is wrong.

Putting people first demands a revolution in lifetime learning because education today is more than the key to climbing the ladder of economic opportunity; it is an imperative for our nation. Our strategy will invest in our people at every stage of their lives. It will put people first by dramatically improving the way parents prepare their children for school, giving students the chance to train for jobs or pay for college, and providing workers with the training and retraining they need to compete and win in tomorrow's economy.

Here's what we must do:

Parents and Children Together

• *Inspire parents to take responsibility and empower them* with the knowledge they need to help their children enter school ready to learn; help disadvantaged parents work with their children to build an ethic of learning at home that benefits both.

• *Fully fund programs* that save us several dollars for every one spent—Head Start, the Women, Infants and Children (WIC) program, and other critical initiatives recommended by the National Commission on Children.

Establishing Tough Standards

• Work with educators, parents, business leaders, and public officials to create a set of *national standards* for what students should know.

• Create a *national examination system* to measure

our students' and schools' progress in meeting the national standards.

• *Achieve the 1989 Education Summit's "National Education Goals"* by the year 2000: every child should begin school physically and mentally ready to learn; our high school graduation rate should rise from 71 to 90 percent, the current international standard; and students should be knowledgeable in math, science, language, history, and geography when they graduate high school.

Reforming Our Schools

• Reduce the education gap between rich and poor students by increasing Chapter One funding for low-income students and by giving schools greater flexibility to spend the money in ways they think most effective, like *reducing class sizes in early grades.*

• Grant *expanded decision-making powers at the school level*—empowering principals, teachers, and parents with increased flexibility in educating our children.

• Support *better incentives to hire and keep good teachers,* including alternative certification for those who want to take up teaching as a second career and differential pay to attract and retain educators in shortage areas like math and science, in urban schools, and in isolated or rural schools.

• Help states develop *public school choice* programs like Arkansas's with protection from discrimination based on race, religion, or income.

Making Our Schools Safe Again

• *Get drugs out of our schools:* work with states and local communities to bring parents, educators, students, law enforcement personnel, and community service workers together to provide comprehensive drug education, prevention, intervention, and treatment programs.

• We would also *support a Safe Schools Initiative,* which will provide funds for violence-ridden schools to hire security personnel and purchase metal detectors, and help cities and states use community policing to put more police officers on the streets in high-crime areas where schools are located.

Alternative and Continuing Education Programs

• Help communities open centers that give dropouts a second chance through a *Youth Opportunity Corps.* Teenagers will be matched with adults who care about them and who will help them develop self-discipline and valuable skills.

• Bring business, labor, and education leaders together to develop a *national apprenticeship-style program* that offers non-college-bound students valuable skills training, with the promise of good jobs when they graduate.

• Maintain the Pell grant program, scrap the existing student loan program, and *establish a National Service Trust Fund* to guarantee every American who wants a college education the means to obtain one. Those who borrow from the fund will pay it back either as a small percentage of their income over time, or through community service as teachers, law enforcement officers, health-care workers, or peer counselors helping kids stay off drugs and in school.

• Invest in *worker retraining programs* that require employers to spend 1.5 percent of payroll for continuing education and training for all workers, not just executives.

Energy

FOR TWELVE YEARS, the Republicans in Washington have undermined our national security and cut short our economic growth because they haven't had a national energy policy. In the last decade, 8000 of our independent oil and gas producers have closed their doors; 300,000 Americans have lost their jobs. Of 4500 domestic drilling rigs operating in the United States in 1981 when Ronald Reagan and George Bush took office, less than 700 remain in operation today. We've fallen behind our competitors in energy efficiency and are in danger of leaving future generations of Americans in a precarious position of overwhelming debt and dependence.

America needs a national energy policy that lets Americans control America's energy future. Instead of coddling special interests whose fortunes depend on America's addiction to foreign oil, our national energy policy will promote national security, energy diversity, economic prosperity, and environmental protection.

It's time to make the right energy choices.

Here's how:

Increase Energy Efficiency and Conservation

• *Increase corporate average fuel economy standards* from the current 27.5 miles per gallon to 40 miles per gallon by the year 2000, and 45 miles per gallon by 2015.

• Develop and implement revenue-neutral market incentives that *reward conservation and penalize polluters and energy-wasters.*

• Adopt transportation strategies and highway spending programs that *encourage car-pooling, high-efficiency highway technology, and mass transit* by including conservation incentives in the federal matching fund program.

• *Promote changes in utility regulation to make energy efficiency profitable* for both utilities and customers.

• *Strengthen federal programs to encourage energy-efficient housing;* encourage state and local governments to adopt building codes that encourage conservation by calling for thicker walls and windows, new compact fluorescent bulbs, more efficient insulation, and new low-cost housing construction that could cut domestic energy consumption by 25 percent using measures that would pay for themselves in five to seven years.

• *Increase energy efficiency in every federal agency* and set standards to ensure that federal grants, contracts, and projects support America's national conservation goals.

Increase Natural Gas Use

• *Implement policies to expand markets for natural gas in every sector*—homes, businesses, industry, electrical generation, and transportation.

• *Speed development and certification of new natural*

gas pipelines to get natural gas to market, with special emphasis on areas not currently adequately served by natural gas.

• *Convert the enormous federal vehicle fleet to natural gas.*

• Use federal research and development dollars to *develop new natural gas applications.*

Expand the Use of Renewable Energy Sources

• *Create a civilian advanced research agency* that will support civilian research and development of *renewable technologies and renewable fuel programs.*

• Reorient the mission of hundreds of national laboratories, moving from defense R&D to *more work on commercial renewable energy projects.*

• Change the tax code to *create greater incentives for renewable energy use.*

• *Give incentives to utilities to adopt least-cost planning,* which factors environmental, social, and economic costs into fuel-use decisions. Least-cost planning is currently employed by utility companies in seventeen states.

A Safe, Environmentally Sound Energy Policy

• *Oppose increased reliance on nuclear power.* There is good reason to believe that we can meet future energy needs—with conservation and the use of alternative fuels—without having to face the staggering costs, delays and uncertainties of nuclear waste disposal.

• *Oppose federal excise gas tax increases.* Instead of a backbreaking federal gas tax, we should try conservation, increased use of natural gas, and increased use of alternative fuels.

• *Prohibit drilling in the Arctic National Wildlife Refuge (ANWR) in Alaska.* Work instead to expand the ANWR to include the 1.5 million-acre Arctic Coastal Plain while ensuring that Native Americans are able to use these lands for traditional subsistence hunting and fishing. Increased energy efficiency and the use of natural gas currently available in the lower forty-eight states can easily negate the need for ANWR drilling.

Environment

FOR ALL ITS rhetoric, the Bush Administration has been an environmental disaster. The President has ignored the threat of global warming and the depletion of the earth's ozone layer, undermined enforcement of the Clean Air Act, supported drilling in Alaska's precious Arctic National Wildlife Refuge, abandoned his "no net loss" wetlands policy, and opposed efforts to increase recycling. The United States ought to lead the world in fighting for environmental protection, but George Bush has been dragging his feet at international environment summits and ignoring his promises here at home.

It's time for a change. We want to give America a real environmental policy. We believe that environmental protection is fundamental to America's national security—and that we must reject Bush Administration attempts to force a false choice between environmental protection and economic growth. A Clinton–Gore Administration will challenge Americans and demand responsibility at every level—from individuals and families to corporations and government agencies—to do more to preserve our world. We will renew America's commitment to leave our children a better nation—a nation whose air, water, and land are unspoiled, whose natural beauty is undimmed, and whose leadership for sustainable global growth is unsurpassed.

We need to adopt an aggressive market-based national strategy to cut pollution and slow the generation of solid waste. We also need to take more effective measures to clean up the pollution and waste that have already harmed our environment. The American people deserve an Administration that cares as much about America's environment and natural heritage as they do.

There are some threats that the American people can't fight alone. The world faces a crisis because of global climate change, ozone depletion, and unsustainable population growth. These developments threaten our fundamental interests—and we must fight them at a global level. America must lead the world, not follow.

Here's what a Clinton–Gore Administration will do:

Pursue Four Goals

• Reduce solid and toxic waste and air and water pollution to ensure we leave our nation cleaner and healthier.
• Preserve places of natural beauty and ecological importance—such as our national parks, wilderness areas, old growth forests, and wetlands—so that we can pass on America's natural splendor to our children.
• Shatter the false choice between environmental protection and economic growth by creating a market-based environmental protection strategy that rewards conservation and "green" business practices while penalizing polluters.
• Exert international leadership to advance our own nation's interest in a healthier global environment, a sta-

ble global climate, and global biodiversity. Reduce American and worldwide use of fossil fuels and airborne chemicals that destroy the ozone layer and work to keep our world's delicate environment in balance.

Reduce Pollution and Solid Waste

• Create and expand markets for recycled products by providing *revenue-neutral tax incentives* that favor the use of recycled materials whenever possible.

• *Create a solid waste reduction program* which gives credits to companies that recover a portion of the waste they generate and penalizes companies that fail to do so. Less efficient companies would be forced to buy waste credits from more efficient companies, creating a strong profit incentive for reducing solid waste.

• *Pass a new Clean Water Act* with standards for "non-point-source" pollution and incentives for our firms, farmers, and families to develop ways to reduce and prevent polluted run-off at its source; launch a national education campaign to encourage all citizens to drastically reduce their contributions to non-point-source pollution made by household chemicals, lawn products, and pesticides.

• *Reform and ensure proper and effective enforcement of the EPA Superfund* so that taxpayer money goes toward cleaning up toxic waste instead of paying legal bills. Currently, almost half of all federal Superfund appropriations go to pay lawyers' fees—while 22,000 Superfund sites threaten the health of citizens and communities across America.

• Support legislation that *allows ordinary citizens to*

sue federal agencies that ignore environmental laws and regulations designed to preserve our environment—so government bureaucrats are made accountable for proper and effective environmental law enforcement.

• Support efforts to *mandate public reporting on toxic chemicals used and produced by companies,* and require those companies to develop plans for reducing their toxic chemical use.

• *Crack down on environmental crime* by holding companies and polluters responsible for their behavior. Corporations that deliberately violate environmental laws will pay the price—and polluters will be sent to jail where appropriate.

Preserve America's Natural Beauty and Key Resources

• *Preserve our ancient forests* for their scientific and ecological importance.

• *Make the "no net loss" wetlands pledge a reality;* base wetlands policy on science instead of politics by working with the National Academy of Sciences and other members of the scientific community to devise appropriate policies. Our wetlands act as a natural filter for much of the water America drinks and make up one of our most important and fragile natural habitats.

• Rededicate the agencies that manage our national parks and wilderness lands to a *true conservation ethic;* expand our efforts to acquire new parklands and recreational sites with funds already available under the federal *Land and Water Conservation Fund.*

• *Designate the Arctic National Wildlife Refuge as a*

wilderness area and stop the crusade for new offshore drilling.

Use Market Forces to Encourage Environmental Protection

• Place *greater emphasis on preventing and reducing pollution* before it happens, so we won't have to spend so much on cleaning it up after the fact. We can do that without big bureaucracies and public spending—by harnessing market forces, integrating environmental incentives into daily production decisions of big firms, and making polluters pay.

• Harness market forces *to reward consumers and businesses that conserve and to penalize polluters and inefficient energy users.*

• Create revenue-neutral tax incentives to encourage the use of *alternative fuels* like natural gas and *renewable energy sources* like hydroelectricity, solar power, and wind power.

Exert American Leadership for a Healthier World

• Provide *real international leadership* to protect the world's delicate environmental balance.

• *Limit U.S. carbon dioxide emissions to 1990 levels* by the year 2000 and accelerate the phase-out of substances that deplete the ozone layer.

• Call on major banks and multinational institutions to negotiate *debt-for-nature swaps* with all developing nations that allow Third World countries to reduce their crippling debt burdens by setting aside precious lands.

- Restore U.S. funding for the *United Nation's population stabilization efforts,* and allow U.S. foreign aid to support international family planning services.
- Explore partnerships and joint ventures with developing countries *to preserve and protect rainforests* while accelerating important medical and agricultural research and development.

Improve Energy Efficiency

- Accelerate our progress toward more fuel-efficient cars, and *raise the Corporate Average Fuel Efficiency (CAFE) standards for automakers to 40 miles per gallon by the year 2000, and 45 miles per gallon by 2015.*
- *Increase U.S. reliance on natural gas*—which is inexpensive, clean-burning and abundant, and can reduce carbon dioxide emissions—by issuing an executive order to purchase natural-gas-powered vehicles for the federal automobile fleet, following Texas's lead.
- *Invest more in the development of renewable energy sources;* encourage the use of new energy sources like wind and solar power, and new methods to make better use of the resources we already have.
- Stop spending 60 percent of the Department of Energy's budget on nuclear weapons, with nuclear power and fossil fuels receiving most of the rest.
- Convert some of our Cold War military spending to civilian purposes, *like funding light rail systems,* which can speed travel, save fuel, and provide transportation for people less able to afford it.
- *Improve America's overall energy efficiency by 20 percent by the year 2000* by making energy conservation

and efficiency central goals in every policy field—in planning communities, designing offices, developing transportation, and regulating utilities.

• Sustain efforts to improve the efficiency of coal operations through development and *use of clean coal technologies.*

Families

Over the past twelve years, Washington has abandoned working families, forcing millions to run harder and harder just to stay in place. While taxes fall and incomes rise for those at the top of the totem pole, middle-class families work harder for less money and pay more taxes to a government that fails to produce what we need: good jobs in a growing economy, world-class education, affordable health care, and safe streets and neighborhoods.

The Republicans have lectured America on the importance of family values. But their policies have made life harder for working families: they have forced parents to choose between the jobs they need and the families they love. They have slashed funding for programs that prepare kids for kindergarten or send teens on to college. They have stood idly by as neighborhoods collapse, violent crime rises, and health costs skyrocket.

A Clinton–Gore Administration will demand more from families, but it will offer more, too. We will demand that parents pay the child support they owe. But we will offer their children the pre-schooling they need. We will demand that young people stay in school and off drugs. But we will offer all Americans safer streets and the chance to borrow for college. Our Administration will demand that people work hard and play by the rules. We will honor and reward those who do.

We cannot afford another four years of a President who doesn't have a plan to help America's families and who backs down from the promises he does make. It is time for a change—time to put people first.

Here's how:

Treat Families Right

• *Grant additional tax relief to families with children.*
• *Sign into law the Family and Medical Leave Act,* which George Bush vetoed in 1990, so that no worker is forced to choose between keeping his or her job and caring for a newborn child or sick family member.
• Create a *child-care network* as complete as the public school network, tailored to the needs of working families; give parents choices between competing public and private institutions.
• Establish more *rigorous standards for licensing child-care facilities* and implement improved methods for enforcing them.
• *Crack down on deadbeat parents* by reporting them to credit agencies, so they can't borrow money for themselves when they're not taking care of their children. Use the Internal Revenue Service to collect child support, start a national deadbeat databank, and make it a felony to cross state lines to avoid paying support.

Educate Our Children

• Send children to school ready to learn by *fully funding pre-school programs* which save us several dollars for every one we spend—Head Start, the Women, Infants and Children (WIC) program, and other critical initiatives recommended by the National Commission on Children.

• Develop national parenting programs like Arkansas's Home Instructional Program for Pre-school Youngsters to *help disadvantaged parents work with their children* to build an ethic of learning at home that benefits both.

• *Dramatically improve K–12 education* by establishing tough standards and a national examination system in core subjects, leveling the playing field for disadvantaged students, and reducing class sizes.

• Give every parent the right to *choose the public school his or her child attends,* as they have in Arkansas; in return, demand that parents work with their children to keep them in school, off drugs, and headed toward graduation.

• *Establish a Youth Opportunity Corps* to give teenagers who drop out of school a second chance. Community youth centers will match teenagers with adults who care about them, and will give kids a chance to develop self-discipline and skills.

• *Give every American the right to borrow for college* by maintaining the Pell grant program, scrapping the existing student loan program, and establishing a National Service Trust Fund. Those who borrow from the fund will be able to repay the balance either as a small percentage of their earnings over time, or through community service—as teachers, law enforcement officers, health-care workers, or peer counselors helping kids stay off drugs and in school.

Guarantee Every Family the Right to Quality, Affordable Health Care

• Control costs, improve quality and cover everybody under a *national health-care plan* that requires insurers to offer a core benefits package, including pre-natal care and other important preventive treatments.

• *Take on the insurance industry* by simplifying financial and accounting procedures; banning underwriting practices that waste billions trying to discover which patients are bad risks; and prohibiting companies from denying coverage to individuals with pre-existing conditions.

• *Stop drug price gouging* by eliminating tax breaks for drug companies that raise their prices faster than Americans' incomes rise.

Make Our Homes, Streets, and Schools Safe Again

• Crack down on violence against women and children by *signing the Violence Against Women Act*, which would provide tougher enforcement and stiffer penalties to deter domestic violence.

• *Put 100,000 new police officers on the streets* by establishing a National Police Corps drawn partly from military veterans and active military personnel.

• *Expand community policing* to stop crimes before they happen by taking officers out of patrol cars and putting them back on the beat.

• Sign the Brady Bill to *create a waiting period for handgun purchases* and allow authorities to conduct background checks to prevent guns from falling into the wrong hands; work to ban assault rifles, which have no legitimate hunting purpose.

• *Launch a Safe Schools Initiative* to help schools take back their facilities as places of learning: make schools eligible for federal assistance to pay for metal detectors and security personnel if they need them; encourage states to get tougher with in-school crime; and fund mentoring, counseling, and outreach programs so kids in trouble with crime, drugs, or gangs have some place to turn.

Reward Working Families

• *Expand the Earned Income Tax Credit* to guarantee a "working wage" so that no American with a family who works full-time is forced to live in poverty.

• *Put an end to welfare as we know it* by making welfare a second chance, not a way of life; *empower people* on welfare with the education, training, and child care they need, for up to two years, so they can break the cycle of dependency—after that, those who can work will have to find a job either in the private sector or in community service.

Gun Control

EVERY YEAR, more than 20,000 Americans are killed with handguns, and many thousands more are injured. A large and growing number of these victims are killed by semiautomatic assault weapons, which have no legitimate sporting purpose. The streets of our cities have become gun bazaars. We must make them safe again.

The large majority of gun owners, however, are law-abiding citizens who use their guns in a responsible manner. As sportsmen, we know that the Constitution guarantees an individual's basic right to keep and bear arms, and we will uphold that right. But too many kids have too many guns in their hands on our cities' streets today. No nation should permit its children to walk around with guns.

We must:

Support the Brady Bill

• Sign the Brady Bill, which would mandate a *waiting period for handgun purchases* to allow police sufficient time to determine whether intended purchasers are underage or have criminal backgrounds, drug histories, or mental health histories.

Ban Assault Weapons

- *Ban semiautomatic assault weapons,* which have no legitimate hunting purpose, and support the right of local law enforcement officials to ban such weapons when gangs move into their neighborhoods.
- *Limit access to multiple-round clips* like the ones used in the tragic killings in Killeen, Texas.

Get Tough on Crime

- Create a National Police Corps and offer veterans and active military personnel a chance to become law enforcement officers at home. This will *add 100,000 new police officers to the streets.*
- Enact *tougher sentences* for criminals who use guns.
- Implement a federal *program for safe schools* so children can concentrate on learning.
- Create *"boot camps"* for first-time nonviolent offenders.
- Develop *strong anti-gang initiatives* and empower public housing residents to get rid of drug dealers.

Health Care

THE AMERICAN health-care system costs too much and does not work. It leaves 60 million Americans without adequate health insurance and bankrupts our families, our businesses, and our federal budget. Instead of putting people first, Washington favors the insurance companies, the drug companies, and the health-care bureaucracies. The most advanced health-care system in the world is being strangled.

And working Americans are paying the price. Since 1980, the average cost of individual health insurance rose from $1000 to $3000 a year. Today health-care costs are the number one cause of labor disputes, bankruptcies, and growth in the federal deficit. People can't change jobs because insurance companies will deny them coverage claiming pre-existing conditions. Small businesses are caught between going broke and doing right by their employees. Drug companies raise prices three times faster than inflation. Working men and women are forced to pay more while their employers cover less.

Health care should be a right, not a privilege. And it can be. We are going to preserve what's best in our system: your family's right to choose who provides care and coverage, American innovation and technology, and the world's best private doctors and hospitals. But we will take on the bureaucracies and corporate interests to make health care affordable and accessible for every American.

We can't afford four more years without a President with a plan and the will to guarantee affordable, quality health care for every American. The United States is the only advanced country in the world without a national health-care plan.

In the first year of a Clinton–Gore Administration, that will change. We will send a national health-care plan to Congress, and we will fight to pass it. No American family should have to go from the doctor's office to the poorhouse.

Here's what we'll do:

Cap National Spending to Control Health-Care Costs

- *Create a health standards board* made up of consumers, providers, business, labor, and government. The health standards board will establish an annual health budget for the nation to limit both public and private expenditures.
- *Crack down on billing fraud* and eliminate incentives that invite abuse.

Take On the Insurance Industry

- Ban underwriting practices that waste billions trying to discover which patients are bad risks; *prohibit companies from denying coverage to individuals with pre-existing conditions.*
- *Protect small businesses through "community rat-*

ings," which requires insurers to spread risks evenly among all companies.

• *Shut down the "paper hospital"* and replace expensive and complex financial forms and accounting procedures with a simplified, streamlined billing system with one claim form. Under the current system, 1500 companies waste millions of dollars processing 1500 sets of forms.

• *Work to provide everyone with "smart cards"* coded with personal medical information.

Stop Drug Price Gouging

• To *protect American consumers* and bring down prescription drug prices, eliminate tax breaks for drug companies that raise their prices faster than Americans' incomes rise.

• Discourage drug companies from spending more on marketing than on *research and development*—because saving lives must come before making money.

Establish a Core Benefits Package

• Through the health standards board, guarantee a *basic health benefits package* that includes ambulatory physician care, inpatient hospital care, prescription drugs, and basic mental health services. The package will also include expanded preventive treatments such as pre-natal care, mammograms, and routine health screenings.

• *Allow consumers to choose* where they receive care to ensure a better fit between provider strengths and consumer needs.

• Expand Medicare for elderly and disabled Americans to include *more long-term care;* place special emphasis on home- and community-based care; and make funding flexible so that those who need care can decide what serves them best.

Develop Health Networks

• Give consumers *access to a variety of local health networks*—made up of insurers, hospitals, clinics, and doctors—to end the costly duplication of services and encourage the shared use of key technologies.

• Allocate to networks a fixed amount of money for each consumer, giving the networks *the necessary incentive to control costs.*

Guarantee Universal Coverage

• Guarantee every American a *core benefits package* set by the health standards board either through his or her employer or by buying into a high-quality public program. No one will be cut off, canceled, denied, or forced to accept inferior care.

• *Limit costs for small employers* by allowing them to group together and form larger groups to purchase less costly health insurance, or to buy into the public program if it is the cheapest option.

• *Phase in business responsibilities,* covering employees through the public program until the transition is complete.

• *Improve preventive and primary care* through community-based health solutions. A successful health plan must provide all Americans with adequate access to health facilities. Our plan will expand school-based clinics and community health centers in medically underserved areas.

Housing

HOME OWNERSHIP and decent housing are essential parts of the American Dream. But for too many Americans, that dream is unobtainable.

Home prices have climbed out of the reach of middle-class Americans. Affordable housing is too difficult to find for the working poor and urban residents. During the Reagan–Bush years, federal appropriations for low-income housing assistance have been slashed, contributing to a massive housing shortage. Millions of Americans have been left homeless on our streets.

We can reverse this trend by renewing our commitment to provide decent, safe, and affordable homes to all Americans, and by forging a new alliance between federal officials, local community leaders, residents, and housing professionals. We must put our people first.

Here's what we must do:

Make Home Ownership a Reality

• *Raise the ceiling on FHA mortgage insurance* to 95 percent of the price of a home in an average metropolitan area. The increase will enable half a million American families to buy their first homes.

• Make home ownership possible for more Americans

through *federal support for low-income, long-term housing buyout programs,* like Tampa's innovative Resurrection of Affordable Housing Program. Innovative packages of long-term subsidized financing encourage low-income buyers to purchase, restore, and resell previously condemned housing.

• Require HUD and the Department of Justice's Civil Rights Division to *aggressively enforce existing fair housing civil rights laws,* to open up housing opportunities currently closed by discrimination.

• *Maintain the mortgage revenue bond program* to make affordable housing a reality for thousands of Americans.

Help America's Renters

• *Strengthen the HOME program* by giving more authority and flexibility to the state and local officials who administer it. Congress created HOME in 1990 to provide additional, quality rental housing for low-income Americans, but at the Bush Administration's urging it limited localities' choices in the use of HOME funds.

• *Permanently extend the Low Income Housing Tax Credit* to spur private development of low- and extra-low-income housing; the credit helps produce more than 120,000 homes a year.

Revitalize America Through Community Development

• *Put neighborhoods at the center of our efforts to revitalize America* by coordinating existing housing, education, employment training, health-care, drug treatment and crime prevention programs. Target resources—community by community—to make the most of scarce federal housing funds.

• Create a *nationwide network of community development banks* to provide small loans to low-income businesses and entrepreneurs in the inner cities. These banks will also invest in affordable housing and help mobilize private lenders.

• Create *urban enterprise zones* in stagnant inner cities, but only for companies willing to take responsibility. Business taxes and federal regulations will be minimized to provide incentives to set up shop. In return, companies will have to make jobs for local residents a top priority.

• *Ease the credit crunch* in our inner cities by passing a more progressive Community Reinvestment Act to prevent redlining; require financial institutions to invest in homes in their communities.

Offer New Hope for Low-Income Housing and Public Housing Residents

• *Empower low-income housing residents to expel drug dealers and criminals* from the buildings in which they live: encourage programs like the Chicago Housing Authority's Operation Clean Sweep, which has helped housing residents clean up buildings and kick out criminals; give tenants a greater role in building management to instill pride and responsibility and reduce bureaucracy.

• Preserve our nation's multibillion-dollar investment in public housing by *ensuring that adequate funding for maintenance and upkeep is included in the HUD budget.*

Fight Homelessness

- *Transfer 10 percent of HUD and other government-controlled housing* to community nonprofit organizations and churches to house the homeless.
- *Use the housing available at closed military bases to house the homeless,* giving preference to homeless military veterans.
- *Develop targeted strategies to help different homeless populations*—those who need supported living environments, those who need residential drug and alcohol treatment, and those who need housing for their families because they can't afford it.
- Hold a *Housing and Homelessness Summit* with urban leaders and mayors to create a new consensus for poverty programs, funding levels, and federal assistance for innovative housing crisis solutions.

Immigration

No PART OF the American story is more important to preserve than our rich and proud tradition of responding to the yearnings in all people for personal freedom, political rights, and economic opportunity. The end of the Cold War has not brought an end to persecution or to the plight of refugees. Civil and ethnic strife, repression, poverty, and environmental degradation continue to cause upheavals.

A Clinton–Gore Administration will support policies that promote fairness, nondiscrimination, and family reunification, and reflect our constitutional freedoms of speech, association, and travel. While we must be generous, we cannot admit all who want to come. Priority should be given to family reunification, refugees, and workers whose skills are needed.

We will work to:

Reunite Families

- Make family reunification the cornerstone of American immigration policy.
- Eliminate backlogs that separate husbands and wives and their children. Their present two-year wait for a visa is intolerable.

• Reduce the unreasonable backlog for extended family members—which can be as long as fifteen years.

Support American Workers

• Meet our first obligation—to recruit, train, and maintain the competitiveness of our own workforce, and to ensure that immigration laws do not displace American workers.

• Ensure that temporary worker programs are not used to displace American workers or to undermine our union organizations.

• Maintain immigration laws that enable employers to obtain the workers they need where labor shortages exist.

Fight Discrimination

• Make it a top priority of our Administration to vigorously enforce our labor and antidiscrimination laws.

• Work to get rid of sweat shops and abusive farm labor contractors—not only to help control immigration, but also to help all Americans.

Enforce and Improve Border Controls

• Enhance the enforcement of the laws controlling our borders, and ensure that the human rights of all immigrants are respected.

• Improve the border patrol and ensure that it is held accountable for its actions.

• Provide new technology and training in the latest enforcement techniques.

Improve Domestic Conditions in Latin America

• Develop economic and foreign policies that encourage economic growth in countries where the lack of economic opportunities "pushes out" their residents. By cooperating with our developing allies in ways that treat them as *true partners,* we will reduce the "push" factor.

• Support trade agreements with Latin-American countries that improve and enforce labor, wage, health, safety, and environmental standards at home and abroad. Keep jobs at home and help people abroad live richer, safer lives.

Encourage Immigrant Participation

• Institute public information programs to advise permanent residents of the requirements of citizenship.

• Encourage and assist community organizations to establish education programs to aid legal residents to meet these requirements.

• Ensure that citizenship fees do not pose an undue burden. Keep fees to the minimum necessary to cover costs.

• Work with organizations such as the Southwest Voter Registration and Education Project, the Mexican-American Legal Defense Fund, the National Association of Latino Elected Officials and the Latin American Council of Labor Advancement on issues affecting voter registration and citizenship.

Support Continuing Immigration

• Recognize that even in the post–Cold War era, people still flee political persecution.

• Continue to offer the protection of political asylum regardless of our relationship with the countries fled.

• Encourage democracy and human rights abroad.

• Condition favorable trade terms with repressive regimes, such as China's Communist government, on their respect for human rights, political liberalization, and responsible international conduct.

• Ensure that legitimate claims for asylum are granted and that those denied asylum have received full and fair proceedings.

• Make every effort to support voluntary repatriation after the resolution of conflicts.

• Support the Diversity Visa Program, which reaches out to those unfairly excluded by our immigration policies.

End AIDS Immigration Restrictions

• Stop the cynical politicization of federal immigration policies. Direct the Justice Department to follow the Department of Health and Human Services' recommendation that HIV be removed from the immigration restrictions list.

Stop the Forced Repatriation of Haitian Refugees

• Reverse Bush Administration policy, and oppose repatriation.

• Give fleeing Haitians refuge and consideration for political asylum until democracy is restored to Haiti. Provide them safe haven, and encourage other nations to do the same.

• Seek tightening of the Organization of American States' embargo of Haiti.

• Insist that our European allies observe the embargo, particularly with regard to oil.

• Intensify direct pressure from the United States to restore an elected government.

Help Jews Leave Russia

• As anti-Semitic fervor increases in the former Soviet Union, uphold America's longstanding commitment to freedom of emigration.

• Ensure sufficient support for the 50,000 refugees from the former Soviet Union resettling in the United States each year.

• Support Israel's request for our assistance in resettling hundreds of thousands of Jews from the former Soviet Union. The Bush Administration is wrong to hold hostage to political struggle hundreds of thousands of people whose freedom we have long demanded.

Israel and the Middle East

THE END OF the Cold War does not mean the end of U.S. responsibility abroad, especially in the Middle East. The people of the region are still denied peace and democracy. America's friend, Israel, is still threatened by her neighbors.

The United States has vital interests in the Middle East. That is why we supported President Bush's efforts to throw Saddam Hussein out of Kuwait. We must remain engaged in the region and continue to promote the spread of democracy, human rights, and free markets.

Among all the countries in the Middle East, only Israel has experienced the peaceful transfer of power by ballot—not by bullet. We will never let Israel down.

The Bush Administration has gravely harmed our relationship with Israel. It has wrongly:

- Pressured Israel to make one-sided concessions in the peace process.
- Ignored the cruel and crippling economic boycott of Israel by its Arab neighbors, and disregarded other roadblocks to peace.
- Denied Israel's request for humanitarian assistance in resettling Russian Jews.

- Eroded Israel's security by selling billions of dollars in sophisticated weaponry to its Arab neighbors.

We oppose the Bush Administration's actions. We believe they are no way to treat a steady friend and stable democracy.

Here's what we would do:

Loan Guarantees

We support Israel's long-standing request for our assistance in its effort to cope with the massive influx of Jewish refugees from the former Soviet Union. We will not hold hostage to political struggle hundreds of thousands of men, women, and children whose freedom we've demanded for decades.

Peace Process

The United States will work with the new Israeli government to move the peace process forward. In doing so the United States cannot rightly predetermine the outcome of the negotiations or impose peace on any party.

- We can and should serve as an honest broker and, on occasion, as a catalyst. No side should be expected to make unilateral concessions.
- Jerusalem is the capital of the state of Israel and must remain an undivided city accessible to people of all faiths.
- Peace that does not provide for Israel's security will not be secure and lasting.

Palestinian State

The Palestinians should have the right—as specified in the Camp David accords—to participate in the determination of their future. But they do not have the right to determine Israel's future. For that reason, we oppose the creation of an independent Palestinian state.

Democracy

Our foreign policy must promote democracy as well as stability. We cannot, as the Bush–Quayle Administration has done, ignore the link between the two.

- We should promote democracy in the Middle East and throughout the world. The Bush–Quayle Administration lost an opportunity to promote democracy in Kuwait.
- A Clinton–Gore Administration will never forge strategic relationships with dangerous, despotic regimes. Bush failed to learn from his appeasement of Saddam Hussein when he shared intelligence with him, awarded him credits, and opposed sanctions until the invasion of Kuwait. Today the Bush Administration repeats that mistake as it casts a blind eye on Syria's human-rights abuses and on its support for terrorism.

A Strategic Relationship

The United States has a fundamental interest not only in the security of Israel but also in our two nations' strategic cooperation in the region.

• Unlike the current Administration, our Administration will fulfill American commitments on the prepositioning of military stocks in Israel, and will enhance logistics cooperation to support American forces in the region.

• We understand and firmly support Israel's need to maintain a qualitative military edge over any potential combination of Arab adversaries. We remember the contributions Israel made during the Gulf War—especially the forbearance which was so essential to the successful war effort. We also know that had Israel not conducted its surgical strike against Iraq's nuclear reactor in 1981, our forces might well have confronted a Saddam Hussein armed with nuclear weapons in 1991.

An Economic Partnership

Israel's greatest resource has always been the genius of its people, and America has always benefited from that genius. In 1991, American exports to Israel totaled $3.3 billion, and over the next five years, Israel is expected to purchase as much as $30 billion in American goods—providing needed benefits and jobs to the American economy.

• Together, our two nations should create a Joint American-Israeli High-Tech Commission to work on research and development of the technologies of the twenty-first century.

Against the Arms Race

We learned from Saddam Hussein's conquest of Kuwait that missiles and military dictators are a dangerous combination. It is time we became a leader in the effort to rein in the dangerous proliferation not only of weapons of mass destruction, but of conventional arsenals as well.

• We need to aid Israel's defense against these dangerous weapons by ensuring the completion of the Arrow anti-ballistic missile.

• We need an administration that will produce action, not just promises, to stop the spread of dangerous missiles in the Middle East. We need a strong international effort and tough sanctions to keep weapons of mass destruction out of the hands of tyrants like those in Iran, Iraq, Libya, and Syria.

Labor

IF AMERICA is to regain its competitiveness, we must revitalize the American workplace to increase productivity and expand opportunity. We will not accept four more years in which Americans work longer hours for less money and pay more for health care, housing, and education.

Think what our nation could become if we had the kind of partnership we need: a partnership between business and labor and education and government, committed to compete and win in the global economy.

We are determined to improve education and job training, provide affordable and accessible health care for all Americans, increase worker safety, open foreign markets, and create an environment in which workers at the front lines make decisions instead of simply following orders. We have received the endorsement of the national AFL-CIO and many other unions for our detailed proposals and record on standing up for America's workers.

Our Administration will:

• *Sign the Workplace Fairness Act* to ban permanent replacement of striking workers and preserve the collective bargaining process. We are committed to the rights of working men and women to organize and bargain collectively, and we support the repeal of Section 14b of the Taft-Hartley Act to create a level playing field between labor and management.

- *Guarantee every American affordable, quality health care;* control costs, improve quality, and expand preventive and long-term care by taking on the medical insurance industry and the drug companies.

- *Help workers gain more power* in their companies' day-to-day operations, the organization of their workplaces, and the type of compensation they receive.

- *Improve the quality and efficiency of government* by working closely with public employee unions and organizations like the State Local Government Labor Management Committee to advance a positive understanding of the role of government.

- *Increase the minimum wage* to keep pace with inflation and enforce the prevailing wage protections provided by the Davis-Bacon Act.

- *Expand the Earned Income Tax Credit* to guarantee a "working wage" so that no American who works full-time is forced to live in poverty.

- Eliminate tax deductions for *excessive executive pay.*

- *Stop giving tax breaks* to American companies that shut down their plants here and ship American jobs overseas.

- *Sign into law the Family and Medical Leave Act,* which George Bush vetoed in 1990, to allow workers to take a leave of absence from work when a child is born or when a family member is ill.

- *Provide lifetime training* by requiring every employer to spend 1.5 percent of payroll for continuing education and training for all workers, not just executives.
- *Train non-college-bound youth* for high-wage, high-quality jobs through a national apprenticeship-style program that will pool the expertise of schools, local businesses, and unions.
- *Make adult literacy programs available* by supporting clear and comprehensive state plans to teach everyone with a job to read and give every worker the chance to earn a General Equivalency Diploma.
- *Support a chemical right-to-know law* to inform and protect workers and vigorously enforce worker safety regulations already on the books. Fully enforce Occupational Safety and Health Administration guidelines.
- *Create hundreds of thousands of American jobs by opening up foreign markets* and insisting that our trading partners tear down their trade barriers.
- *Extend unemployment benefits* to jobless workers in the event of a recession.

National Security

WE CANNOT GO four more years without a plan to lead the world. With the end of the Cold War, we need a team in the White House whose goal is not to resist change, but to shape it. The defense of freedom and the promotion of democracy around the world not only reflect our deepest values; they serve our national interest.

We must define a new national security policy to build on the victory of freedom in the Cold War. It must express rights and responsibilities that challenge our people, our leaders, and our allies to work together to build a safer, more prosperous, and more democratic world.

Our vision for U.S. foreign policy is based on a simple premise: at a time of fundamental change, America must lead the world we have done so much to make through foreign policies that address the challenges and opportunities of the next decade. And to provide that leadership we must:

CREATE A SECURITY STRATEGY

- *Rebuild America's economic strength.* We cannot lead abroad if we are weak at home.
- *Remain engaged in the international arena* and

ready to counter threats to stability from former Communist countries and from continuing regional conflicts. The end of the Cold War does not mean the end of threats to our interests. If our challenge is no longer to bear every burden, it is still to tip the balance.

• Use the power of *American values* in shaping the post–Cold War era.

• Guided by these principles, we will pursue three clear objectives: to reestablish America's *economic leadership* at home and abroad, to prepare our *military forces* for a new era, and to encourage the spread and consolidation of *democracy* abroad.

RESTORE AMERICA'S ECONOMIC LEADERSHIP

Our plan to revive America's economic growth will put America back on track and restore America's economic leadership abroad. The job of regaining America's competitive edge begins at home. Economic strength is a central element of our national security policy.

Growth

• Lead the world into a new era of global growth— because without growth abroad, our own economy cannot thrive.

Trade

Open and expanding global markets benefit all Americans. We strongly support free, fair, open, and expanding trade, including the GATT negotiations.

• Avoid protectionism but respond to other nations' unfair trading practices and protect America's interests. Support a strong "Super 301" to achieve that goal.
• Favor free trade agreements, so long as they are fair to American workers and farmers, protect the environment, and promote decent labor standards at home and abroad.

A Technological Edge

The private sector must maintain the initiative, but government has an indispensable role.

• Maintain our ability to compete with Europe and Japan in emerging technologies like biotechnology, superconductors, and computer-integrated manufacturing.
• Utilize the extraordinary talent at our national laboratories to keep the United States at the forefront of civilian and military technology.
• Work with private companies and universities to advance technologies that will improve our lives and create jobs.
• Help develop a commitment between business and labor to make world-class products.
• Create an Economic Security Council, similar to the

National Security Council, to coordinate our international economic policy.

RESTRUCTURE OUR MILITARY FORCES

We will not shrink from using military force responsibly, and a Clinton–Gore Administration will maintain the forces needed to win, and win decisively, should that necessity arise. We supported Operation Desert Storm and the use of force, if necessary, to enforce U.N. resolutions on Iraq and to ensure delivery of humanitarian aid in the former Yugoslavia.

Today's defense debate centers too narrowly on the size of the military budget. The real questions are: What threats do we face? What forces do we need to counter them? How must we change?

A Five-Year Plan

• Maintain military forces—including a survivable nuclear deterrent—strong enough to deter and defeat any threat to our essential interests.

• Set the level of our defense spending based not on old habits but on what we need to protect our interests. We can reduce substantially our military forces and still protect U.S. interests.

• Shift the focus of our conventional forces from defending against Soviet invasion of Western Europe to projecting power whenever and wherever our national interests are threatened.

• Call on our allies to shoulder more of the defense burden.

• Preserve the two attributes that have made the American military the best in the world—the outstanding quality of our personnel and the overwhelming superiority of our technology.

• Enhance our intelligence capabilities to achieve a more sophisticated and accurate understanding of political, economic, and cultural conditions.

Conventional Forces

• Maintain our commitment to NATO as further European security arrangements evolve.

• Meet our NATO responsibilities in Europe with 75,000 to 100,000 U.S. troops, rather than the 150,000 troops now proposed by George Bush.

• Keep U.S. forces in northeast Asia as long as North Korea presents a threat to our South Korean ally.

• Defend the sea lanes and project force with ten carriers rather than twelve.

• Develop greater air and sea lift capacity; among other efforts, produce the C-17 transport aircraft.

• Enhance the rapid deployment capability of our Marines.

Defense Savings

Our defense plan will save more than $100 billion through 1997. The funds we save will be spent on rebuilding America and reducing our deficit. Our cut is $60 billion more over five years than the Cold War budget the Bush Administration still advocates.

- *Force structure:* we can save tens of billions of dollars by developing a smaller force structure, with fewer forces in Europe and a greater orientation to the mobile projection forces needed in the post–Cold War world.
- *SDI:* we should focus our research and development on the goal of a limited missile defense system within the strict framework of the ABM Treaty. Deployment of a massive space-based defense, such as Brilliant Pebbles, is not necessary.
- *Nuclear weapons development:* with smaller nuclear arsenals and no need to develop new nuclear weapons designs, we will curtail spending on nuclear production and testing.
- This *moderate reduction* will enable us to retain our superior technology, high quality personnel, and strong industrial base, and to meet threats that could either increase or decrease in the future.

CONVERT DEFENSE INDUSTRIES

We must not forget the dedicated men and women whose hard work helped win the Cold War.

- Reinvest our military resources in the future of the people who won the Cold War. We need to transfer these immeasurable human resources into our workforce and into our schools.
- Train military personnel for critical civilian professions by expanding the Montgomery GI Bill.

• Create an education fund to provide grants for professionals formerly engaged in defense work.

• Insist on advance notification and help communities plan for a transition from a defense to a domestic economy.

• Preserve the core elements of our defense industrial base to ensure that we can meet the challenges of the future. For example, wind down Seawolf production in a manner that will preserve our crucial submarine construction capability.

• Establish a new advanced research agency—a civilian agency modeled on the Department of Defense's research and development arm, the Defense Advanced Research Projects Agency (DARPA)—that could help provide commercial work for America's scientists and engineers.

SHARE THE BURDEN

While Desert Storm set a useful precedent for cost-sharing, American forces still did most of the fighting and dying within the coalition.

• Work to shift that burden to a wider coalition of nations of which America will be a part.

• Support the recent more active role of the United Nations in troubled spots around the world.

• Pursue the establishment of a voluntary U.N. Rapid Deployment Force to deter aggression, provide humanitarian relief, and combat terrorism and drug trafficking.

STOP WEAPONS

We can do more to stop weapons of mass destruction from spreading.

- Strengthen the International Atomic Energy Agency and lead efforts to enable it to conduct surprise inspections.
- Pursue stricter standards and better verification of the Nuclear Nonproliferation Treaty.
- Work harder to get more countries to join the Missile Technology Control Regime.
- Get tough with countries and companies that sell these technologies and work with all countries for tough, enforceable, international nonproliferation agreements.
- Take the lead in negotiating a Comprehensive Test Ban Treaty through a phased approach.

PROMOTE DEMOCRACY

U.S. foreign policy cannot be divorced from the moral principles most American share. We cannot disregard how other governments treat their own people—whether their domestic institutions are democratic or repressive, whether they help encourage or check illegal conduct beyond their borders. It should matter to us how others govern themselves. Democracy is in our interest.

The end of the Cold War presents America with extraordinary opportunities for economic renewal at home. But that success is directly related to the success of those still struggling for democracy, human rights, and free market economies around the world.

The Need for New Leadership

• President Bush has too often clung to the status quo and hesitated to support democratic forces. His failure to articulate clear goals or a rationale for an engaged foreign policy has fueled a dangerous new isolationism.

• We need new leadership that will stand with the forces of democratic change. We need a President who can set clear goals and explain to the American people the importance of international engagement—a President who will utilize our economic, political, and cultural resources to assist the new forces of freedom emerging around the world.

Failed Bush-Quayle Policies

• The Administration waited too long to recognize and assist the new nations of the former Soviet Union.

• The Administration sat on the sidelines for too long while the former Yugoslavia slipped into chaos and civil war.

• The Administration turned its back on those struggling for democracy in China and on those fleeing Haiti.

• The Administration pressured democratic Israel to make one-sided concessions in the Middle East peace talks, damaging our ability to act as an honest broker.

• The Administration appeased Saddam Hussein when it shared intelligence with him, awarded him credits, and opposed sanctions against him up to the eve of his invasion of Kuwait.

- The Administration is poised to repeat that mistake as it casts a blind eye on Syria's human rights abuses and on its support for terrorism.
- The Administration lost an opportunity to promote democracy in Kuwait.

Engagement for Democracy

A Clinton–Gore Administration will never forge strategic relationships with dangerous, despotic regimes. It will understand that our foreign policy must promote democracy as well as stability. We cannot—as this Administration has too often done—ignore the link between the two. A Clinton–Gore Administration will pursue a foreign policy of Engagement for Democracy. We will:

- Reform our foreign assistance programs in Africa, the Caribbean, Latin America, and elsewhere to ensure our aid promotes democracy, not tyranny.
- Respond more energetically to help the people of the former Soviet empire demilitarize their societies and build free political and economic institutions.
- Firmly support Israel and other democracies which face threats to their security.
- Use our extensive economic and diplomatic leverage to increase material incentives to democratize and to raise the costs for those who don't.
    — Maintain state and local sanctions against South Africa until there is an irreversible, full, and fair

accommodation with the black majority to create a democratic government.

— Toughen sanctions against the de facto government of Haiti until democracy is restored.

— Condition favorable trade terms with repressive regimes—such as China's Communist regime—on respect for human rights, political liberalization, and responsible international conduct.

• Promote democratic development. Support groups like the National Endowment for Democracy and encourage the U.S. Information Agency to channel more of its resources to promoting democracy.

• Establish a Radio Free Asia. Just as Radio Free Europe and Voice of America helped bring the truth to the Communist bloc nations, we should create a Radio Free Asia to carry news and hope to China, Vietnam, and elsewhere.

• Launch a Democracy Corps to send thousands of talented American volunteers to countries that need their legal, financial, and political expertise.

• Support multilateral structures to assist countries struggling with the transition to democracy and the market economy.

• Encourage private investment in the former Soviet Union, not only to help promote reforms, but also to ensure that the United States is not shut out of the region's future lucrative markets.

Older Americans

THE GENERATION that worked its way out of the Great Depression, won the Second World War, and endured the worst of the Cold War has seen harder times than these. But older Americans know that we can do better— by them and by future generations.

The Republicans in Washington have repeatedly tried to cut programs that protect the rights and prosperity of older Americans. We think that's wrong. We will protect the long-term solvency of Social Security, protect the integrity of the Trust Fund, and lift the earnings test limitation.

A Clinton–Gore Administration will also work to enact a national health-care plan in its first year, expand long-term care services, bring down prescription drug costs, and enact family and medical leave legislation to guarantee that working Americans can keep their jobs while they care for ailing parents.

It is time to honor the compact between generations. Here's how:

Social Security

• Our Administration will *protect the integrity of the Social Security system* and ensure that it remains solvent in years to come.

• *Lift the Social Security earnings test limitation* so that older Americans are able to help rebuild our economy and create a better future for all.

National Health Care

• *Guarantee affordable, quality health care* by taking on the insurance industry and drug companies. We will guarantee a core package of benefits for every American.
• *Preserve and protect Medicare benefits.*

Long-term Care

• *Expand choices in care.* We will guarantee older Americans more control of their health care. Options will be expanded to include personal and home care, visiting nurse services, adult day care, and senior center services. Those who need little assistance in daily living will not be forced into nursing homes.
• *Bring down prescription drug prices.* In the last decade, the price of prescription drugs has risen at three times the rate of inflation. Some companies charge Americans more than they charge people from other countries for the same product. We support Sen. David Pryor's proposal to take away tax breaks from drug companies that raise their prices faster than the rate of inflation.

Safe and Strong Communities

• Fight crime by putting *100,000 new police officers* on the streets. We will create a National Police Corps and offer unemployed veterans and active military personnel a chance to become law enforcement officers here at home.

• Provide federal assistance to areas hard hit by crime if they adopt a *comprehensive crime control plan* that includes proven anti-crime measures, such as community-based policing, which puts more police on the beat.

• *Put neighborhoods at the center of our efforts to revitalize America* by coordinating existing housing, education, employment training, health care, drug treatment, and crime prevention programs. We will target resources community by community to make the most of federal housing funds.

• *Strengthen the HOME program* to help community groups provide additional quality rental housing to low-income Americans.

The Family and Medical Leave Act

• *Sign the Family and Medical Leave Act.* This act will allow working parents to take twelve weeks of unpaid leave per year to care for a newborn child or sick family member, including an elderly parent. George Bush vetoed this legislation—leaving the United States as the only industrialized country in the world without a national family and medical leave policy.

Rebuilding America

To BUILD A twenty-first-century economy, America must revive a nineteenth-century habit—investing in the common, national economic resources that enable every person and every firm to create wealth and value. The only foundation for prospering in the global economy is investing in ourselves.

In the 1980s, the concrete foundations of the United States crumbled as the investment gap widened between America and our global competitors. By the decade's end, Japan and Germany were investing more than twelve times what we spend on roads, bridges, sewers, and the information networks and technologies of the future. No wonder they threaten to surpass America in manufacturing by 1996. No wonder we are slipping behind.

Just as interstate highway construction in the 1950s ushered in two decades of unparalleled growth, investing in the pathways of the future will put Americans back to work and spur economic growth. The creation of large, predictable markets will stimulate private industry to invest in our economy, create high-wage jobs, and smooth our transition from a defense to a peacetime economy. The goal: to develop the world's best communication, transportation, and environmental systems—and rebuild America.

Here's what we'll do:

• Create a *Rebuild America Fund,* with a $20 billion federal investment each year for four years—leveraged with state, local, private sector, and pension fund contributions. Make states and localities responsible for project development and management. User fees such as road tolls and solid-waste disposal charges will help guarantee these investments.

• Invest in *transportation* systems: renovate our country's roads, bridges, and railroads; create a high-speed rail network linking our major cities and commercial hubs; develop "smart" highway technology to expand the capacity, speed, and efficiency of our major roadways; and develop high-tech short-haul aircraft.

• Create a door-to-door *information network* to link every home, business, lab, classroom, and library by the year 2015. Put public records, databases, libraries, and educational materials on line for public use to expand access to information.

• Develop new *environmental technologies* and create the world's most advanced systems to recycle, treat toxic waste, and clean our air and water; direct funds to the development of new, clean, efficient energy sources.

• Develop a plan for *defense conversion* to ensure that the communities and millions of talented workers that won the Cold War don't get left out in the cold. Many of the skills and technologies required to rebuild America are similar to those now used in our defense industries. We will encourage companies that bid on projects to rebuild America to contract work to, or purchase, existing defense facilities; order the Pentagon to conduct a national defense-jobs inventory to assist displaced workers; and provide special conversion loans and grants to small business defense contractors.

• Provide tax incentives to companies and entrepreneurs that *invest in America.*

• Utilize the extraordinary talent at our hundreds of national laboratories to *keep the United States at the forefront of civilian and military technology.*

• Work with private companies and universities to advance technologies that improve our lives and create jobs. We will create a *civilian advanced technology agency* modeled after the successful Defense Advanced Research Projects Agency (DARPA). The agency will increase our commercial R&D spending and focus its efforts in crucial new industries such as biotechnology, robotics, high-speed computing, and environmental technology.

Small Business

WE BELIEVE in business. We believe in the marketplace. We know that economic growth will be the best jobs program this country will ever have. Small businesses create most of the new jobs in this country and they need to flourish if we are all to prosper.

America cannot afford another four years without a strategy to make our economy grow again. We must put an end to the era of rewarding outrageous executive pay and shipping American jobs overseas while leaving small businesses without basic support.

A Clinton–Gore Administration will encourage small business people and entrepreneurs to take risks and reward those with the patience, the courage, and the determination to create new jobs. We will provide incentives for those who start new businesses and develop new technologies, and we will make sure that the small defense contractors who helped win the Cold War don't get left out in the cold. Finally, we'll keep health care costs for small businesses down.

America needs a new approach to economics that will give new hope to our people and breathe new life into the American Dream. We need a new national strategy that will reward work and those who play by the rules, and that will expand opportunity for small business and entrepreneurs.

A Clinton–Gore Administration will treat small businesses right. Here's how:

Create Incentives for Small Businesses to Invest

• Offer a *new enterprise tax credit* that provides a 50 percent tax exclusion for those who take risks by making long-term investments in new businesses.

• Provide a *targeted investment tax credit* to encourage investment in new plants and productive equipment here at home that we need to compete in the global economy.

• Make permanent the *research and development tax credit* to reward companies that invest in groundbreaking technologies.

Contain Small Business Health-Care Costs

• Provide affordable, quality *health care for all Americans*, while protecting small businesses from rising health-care costs.

• *Phase in small employer and new business health-care responsibilities* until costs are reduced. In the interim their employees will be covered by the public health-care program with co-payment requirements to discourage overutilization and encourage shared responsibility.

• Stop underwriting practices that divide Americans into small risk groups and raise the cost of health-care coverage for small business. Institute a *broad-based community rating system* to guarantee access, continuity, and renewability of coverage.

• Allow small businesses to buy into a *public health program* if it is less expensive than similar plans offered by private insurers.

• Promote *managed competition* by eliminating barriers to small businesses that want to band together to form larger groups to purchase health insurance at lower prices.

Facilitate Defense Conversion for Small Defense Contractors

• Increase *technical, financial, and marketing assistance to America's small businesses,* which will be critical in the provision of new, high-tech jobs for former small defense contractor employees.

• Provide *small business conversion grants* through the Small Business Administration (SBA) to help small defense contractors finance their transition from defense to civilian production.

• Create a small business *Technical Extension Service,* based on the successful Agriculture Extension and Minnesota's effective Project Outreach Program, to give small businesses easy access to technical expertise. A primary goal of the extension service will be to provide information on marketing, finance, and technology to assist firms converting to civilian production.

• Require the SBA to set aside a percentage of its loan program for *successful small business defense con-*

tractors that are attempting to convert to civilian enterprise.

Increase Small Business Exports and Ensure Fair Trade

• Work to create an open trading system and support efforts to *reduce trade barriers through the General Agreement on Tariffs and Trades (GATT)*.

• Pass a *sharper, stronger "Super 301"* trade bill to encourage our trading partners to permit U.S. goods access to their markets.

• Support a *North American Free Trade Agreement* so long as it provides adequate protection for workers, farmers, and the environment on both sides of the border.

Encourage Small Businesses to Invest in Rural Areas and Inner Cities

• Set up a *national network of small business community development banks* like the South Shore Bank of Chicago and its rural counterpart, the Southern Development Bancorporation in Arkansas, to give low-income entrepreneurs the tools they need to start new businesses. Small business is the key to employment in our cities, and must be encouraged. The South Shore Bank has proven that free enterprise can flourish with the proper financial support in the most challenging of circumstances.

• *Create urban enterprise zones* to encourage investment in inner city development and provide jobs for local residents.

• Rewrite and *pass a stronger Community Reinvest-*

ment Act that challenges banks to lend to entrepreneurs and promotes development projects that reinforce community and neighborhood goals.

• *Support the Minority Small Business Investment Company* and other programs that encourage development of minority-owned small businesses.

Space

THE END OF the Cold War offers new opportunities and new challenges for our civilian space program. In recent years the program has lacked vision and leadership. Because the Reagan and Bush Administrations have failed to establish priorities, and because they have not matched program needs with available resources, the National Aeronautics and Space Administration (NASA) has been saddled with more missions than it can successfully accomplish.

We support a strong U.S. civilian space program—for its scientific value, its economic and environmental benefits, its role in building new partnerships with other countries, and its inspiration of our nation's youth. A Clinton–Gore Administration space program will seek to meet the needs of the United States and other nations while moving toward our long-term space objectives, including human exploration of the solar system. Our space program will also promote the development of new technologies, create new jobs for our highly skilled former defense workers, and increase our understanding of the planet and its delicate environmental balance.

We must:

Move Beyond the Cold War

• *Restore the historical funding equilibrium* between NASA and the Defense Department's space program. The Reagan and Bush Administrations spent more on defense space initiatives than on civilian space projects.

• *Achieve greater cooperation in space* with our traditional allies in Europe and Japan, as well as with Russia. Greater U.S.–Russian cooperation in space will benefit both countries, combining the vast knowledge and resources both countries have gathered since the launch of Sputnik in 1957.

Improve the American Economy Through Space

• Direct NASA to give high *priority to continued improvement of the American civil aircraft industry,* which faces increasing international competition. NASA research can play an important role in developing less polluting, more fuel efficient, and quieter aircraft.

• *Work to improve our space industry's competitiveness.* We'll direct NASA to develop cutting-edge rocket and satellite technologies. We will also develop a new, cost-effective, and reliable launch system to maximize efficiency for scientific and commercial payloads.

Link NASA and the Environment

• Support NASA efforts—like Mission to Planet Earth—to improve our *understanding of the global environment.*

• Call on NASA to develop *smaller, more focused missions* that address pressing environmental concerns.

Strengthen NASA and Education

• *Direct NASA to expand educational programs* that improve American performance in math and science. Space education can help maintain our technological edge and improve our competitiveness.

• Direct NASA to *expand the outreach of its educational efforts* beyond NASA's five field centers, so that millions more young people can learn about space.

Maintain the Space Shuttle and Continue Work on the Space Station

• *Maintain the Space Shuttle's integral role* in our civilian space program. The Shuttle is extremely complex and will always be expensive and difficult to operate. But we must take full advantage of its unique capabilities.

• *Support completion of the space station Freedom,* while basing its development on the twin principles of greater cooperation and burden-sharing with our allies. By organizing effectively on this project, we can pave the way for future joint international ventures, both in space and on earth.

Encourage Planetary Exploration Through the Best Space Science

• *Stress efforts to learn* about other planets. These improve our understanding of our own world and stimulate advances in computers, sensors, image processing, and communications.

• *Fully utilize robotic missions* to learn more about our place in the universe.

• Although we cannot yet commit major resources to *human planetary exploration,* this dream should be among the considerations that guide our science and engineering. Because the entire world would share the benefits of human planetary exploration, the costs for any such project should be borne by other nations as well as the United States.

Trade

To WIN IN global markets, America needs an economic growth plan that provides every person and every firm with the means to be more productive. We need a trade policy that puts people first by investing in ourselves. Our national economic strategy invests in the ongoing education of the American people, in the productive equipment that gives our workers the tools to compete, and in the economic infrastructure that binds our markets and our businesses together. We also recognize that America needs companies that invest in the future, profit from change, and treat their workers as full partners.

When our workers and firms do their part to be competitive, we must have an administration that does its part to ensure that we have open markets for their goods and services. We need a new trade and competitiveness program. A Clinton–Gore Administration will stand up for American workers by standing up to countries that don't play by the rules of free and fair trade. Given a chance, American farmers, workers, and businesses can outcompete anybody.

Our Administration will:

Promote World Growth

To promote world growth policies in the post–Cold War era, we must be economically strong at home. President Bush's weak economic record has deprived him of the authority he needs to insist that Japan adopt expansionary policies to reduce its $100 billion trade surplus, and to ensure that high German interest rates do not cripple growth throughout Europe. A Clinton–Gore Administration will hold all advanced countries accountable for doing their part to promote world trade, end unfair trade practices, and open markets.

Support a Strong "Super 301"

This is the provision of U.S. trade law that has helped to pry open foreign markets. Our competitors need to know that we won't stand for unfair trade practices that prevent our farmers, workers, and businesses from selling products abroad and creating jobs at home. We have had plenty of empty promises on trade; what we need now are results.

Support a North American Free Trade Agreement

We will support a free trade agreement with Mexico so long as it provides adequate protection for workers, farmers, and the environment on both sides of the border. A Clinton–Gore Administration will support a free trade policy that puts people first. We must have strong transition strategies that ensure that workers benefit from a more open world trading system.

Promote GATT

America needs leadership to break the logjam and get the Uruguay Round finished. President Bush's ill-fated trip to Japan and his poor performance at the G-7 summit demonstrate that our trade policies suffer from a lack of presidential leadership. We will ensure that the Uruguay Round opens markets for agriculture, services, and, in particular, manufacturing; protects our intellectual property; and takes a tough stand against unfair trade practices. The United States needs to continue to promote free trade that aims to raise—not lower—standards for health, safety, and the environment. We also believe that no trade agreement should preclude the United States from enforcing nondiscriminatory laws and regulations affecting health, worker safety, and the environment. We will not allow the Uruguay Round to alter U.S. laws and regulations through the back door.

Create an Economic Security Council

A Clinton–Gore Administration will create an Economic Security Council, similar in status to the National Security Council, to coordinate American international economic policy.

Reevaluate MFN with China

We believe that the Bush Administration erred by extending Most Favored Nation trade status to the People's Republic of China before it achieved documented progress on human rights. We should not reward China with improved trade status when it has continued to trade goods made by prison labor and has failed to make sufficient progress on human rights since the Tiananmen Square massacre.

Reform the Office of the U.S. Trade Representative

A Clinton–Gore Administration will issue an executive order banning trade negotiators from cashing in on their positions by serving as representatives of foreign corporations or governments. We will rededicate the Office of the Trade Representative to serving the country—not selling out for lucrative lobbying paychecks from foreign competitors.

Create a Civilian Advanced Technology Agency Modeled on the Defense Advanced Research Projects Agency (DARPA)

America can no longer afford to get the Nobel Prizes while our competitors get the profits. A civilian technology agency will bring businesses and universities together to develop cutting-edge products and technologies, to move our ideas into the marketplace where they can create jobs for our people. The new agency will increase America's commercial R&D spending and focus its efforts in crucial new technologies such as biotechnology, robotics, high speed computing, and environmental technology.

Provide Incentives for Manufacturing Innovation

A Clinton–Gore Administration will dramatically increase incentives for innovation. We will:

• Provide a targeted investment tax credit to encourage investment in the new plants and productive equipment here at home that we need to compete in the global economy.

• Make permanent the research and development tax credit to reward companies that invest in groundbreaking technologies.

• Help small businesses and entrepreneurs by offering a 50 percent tax exclusion to those who take risks by making long-term investments in new businesses.

Stand Up for America's Workers

• Require every employer to spend 1.5 percent of payroll for continued education and training, and make them provide the training to all workers, not just executives.

• Bring business, labor, and education leaders together to develop a national apprenticeship-style system that offers non-college-bound students training in valuable skills.

• Provide all Americans with affordable, quality health care.

• Limit deductions for outrageous executive pay. Companies will be allowed to deduct bonuses tied to profits for top executives only if other employees also receive bonuses.

• Restore the link between pay and performance by

encouraging companies to provide for employee ownership and profit sharing for all employees, not just executives.

• End tax breaks for American companies that shut down their plants here and ship American jobs overseas.

Veterans

FOR DECADES Americans struggled and sacrificed to defend freedom and democracy, and to win the Cold War. Our nation owes a great debt of gratitude to the soldiers, sailors, Marines, airmen, and airwomen whose talent and dedication led to our victory.

We have consistently supported veterans. We deeply appreciate the sacrifices of those who were called to serve our country and fight for the ideals for which it stands. Our veterans deserve only the best.

A Clinton–Gore Administration will work to improve health services at VA hospitals and preserve them strictly for veterans. We must ensure that men and women in the armed services and the defense industries have opportunities to shift their talents to the civilian sector. We offer a detailed plan to utilize their talents and energies to meet our pressing needs at home in the fields of medicine, education, law enforcement, and industrial technology.

Here's what we need to do:

Health Care

• *Appoint a Secretary of Veterans Affairs* who understands the real problems facing veterans and can go directly to the President to cut through bureaucracy and improve services for our veterans.

• *Ensure that the VA receives the funding it needs* to provide excellent, timely care to veterans and *oppose opening VA hospitals up to nonveterans.*

• *Cut bureaucracy* at the VA to decrease waiting periods for outpatient services and to ensure that benefits arrive on time.

• Ensure *advance notification of any changes in benefits packages* and programs for disabled veterans.

• Fund programs to deal with the common *mental health* problems of veterans, such as post-traumatic stress syndrome.

Employment in a Post–Cold War Economy

• *Gradually scale down our military forces* by shifting military personnel from active duty to the National Guard and reserves and gradually limit recruitment and reenlistment efforts.

• *Provide early retirement incentives,* with a prorated pension for military personnel with fifteen to twenty years of service to encourage voluntary military downsizing.

• Work with states to provide *alternative certification programs* for military personnel who retire to take jobs in critical professions like education, health care, or law enforcement, and increase their military credit by one year for each year of such employment.

• *Train military personnel* for critical civilian professions by allowing them to take a one-year educational leave of absence with pay before officially beginning their retirement.

Taking Care of Our Soldiers

• *Expand veterans centers* to help veterans, their spouses, children, and other family members learn to deal with the scars of war.

• *Assist homeless veterans by converting closed military bases to homeless shelters,* with priority for veterans. These centers should provide medical care, job training, and job counseling.

• *Make resolution of the POW/MIA issue a national priority* by insisting on a full accounting of all POWs and MIAs before normalizing relations with Vietnam, working with the Russian government to reveal any information it has on Americans held, and declassifying pertinent government documents.

• *Reevaluate the discharge process,* particularly as it affects Vietnam veterans and the enforcement of the statute of limitations.

Welfare and Work

FOR TWELVE YEARS the Republicans in Washington have praised the virtue of hard work, but they have hurt hardworking Americans. They have talked about "family values," but their policies show they don't really value families. They have pledged to reform welfare, but they have no plan to put people back to work. They have put their elections first—and people last.

Millions of Americans have paid the price. Wages are flat, good jobs are scarce, and poverty has exploded. Today almost one of every five people who works full-time doesn't earn enough to keep his or her family above the poverty level. Almost one of every five children lives in poverty—a million more than ten years ago. And because of deadbeat spouses, more than one of every five single parents doesn't get adequate child support.

It's time to honor and reward people who work hard and play by the rules. That means ending welfare as we know it—not by punishing the poor or preaching to them, but by empowering Americans to take care of their children and improve their lives. No one who works full-time and has children at home should be poor anymore. No one who can work should be able to stay on welfare forever.

We can provide opportunity, demand responsibility,

and end welfare as we know it. We can give every American hope for the future.

Here's how:

End Welfare as We Know It

• *Empower people* with the education, training, and child care they need for up to two years, so they can break the cycle of dependency; expand programs to help people learn to read, get their high school diplomas or equivalency degrees, and acquire specific job skills; and ensure that their children are cared for while they learn.

• After two years, *require those who can work to go to work,* either in the private sector or in community service; provide placement assistance to help everyone find a job, and give the people who can't find one a dignified and meaningful community service job.

• Actively *promote state models that work,* like Arkansas's Project Success.

• Guarantee *affordable, quality health care to every American*—so nobody is forced to stay on welfare because going back to work would mean losing medical insurance.

• *Sign into law the Family and Medical Leave Act,* which President Bush has vetoed, to give workers the right to take twelve weeks of unpaid leave per year to care for a newborn or a sick family member—a right enjoyed by workers in every other advanced industrial nation.

Guarantee a Working Wage

• *Expand the Earned Income Tax Credit* so that no one with a family who works full-time has to raise his or her children in poverty; make up the difference between a family's earnings and the poverty level.

• Increase the minimum wage to keep pace with inflation and enforce the prevailing wage protections contained in the Davis-Bacon Act.

• Create a *national apprenticeship-style program* by bringing business, labor, and education leaders together to offer non-college-bound students valuable skills training, with the promise of good jobs when they graduate.

• Require every employer to spend 1.5 percent of payroll for *continuing education and training* and provide training to all workers, not just executives.

Help Low-Income Americans Build Savings

• Enable low-income Americans to set up *Individual Development Accounts* to save for specific purposes such as post-secondary education, home ownership, retirement, and small business startups.

• *Eliminate foolish regulations* that discourage people receiving income maintenance from saving. It's a travesty that people on welfare who want to do right by themselves and their families can't because the government won't let them.

Stimulate Investment in Inner City and Rural Areas

• Establish a *nationwide network of community development banks,* modeled on the successful South Shore Bank in Chicago and Southern Development Bancorporation in Arkansas, to provide loans to low-income entrepreneurs and homeowners in the inner cities. These banks will also provide advice and assistance to entrepreneurs, invest in affordable housing, and help mobilize private lenders.

• Create *urban enterprise zones* in stagnant inner cities, but only for companies willing to take responsibility. Minimize business taxes and federal regulations to provide incentives to set up shop. In return, require companies to make jobs for local residents a top priority.

• *Ease the credit crunch in our inner cities* by passing a more progressive Community Reinvestment Act to prevent redlining, and by requiring financial institutions to invest in their communities.

Educate Our Children

• Expand innovative parenting programs like Arkansas's Home Instructional Program for Pre-school Youngsters (HIPPY), which helps disadvantaged parents work with their children to *build an ethic of learning at home* that benefits both.

• *Fully fund Head Start,* WIC, and other initiatives recommended by the National Commission on Children that will help send our children to school ready to learn— programs that save the government several dollars for every one it spends.

• *Make educational opportunity a reality* by increasing Chapter One funding for schools in disadvantaged neighborhoods, setting tough standards, and helping communities open youth opportunity centers for dropouts who need a second chance.

• *Give every American the right to borrow money for*

college by maintaining the Pell grant program, scrapping the existing student loan program, and establishing a National Service Trust Fund. Those who borrow from the fund will be able to choose how to repay the balance: either as a small percentage of their earnings over time, or by serving their communities doing work their country needs.

Crack Down on Deadbeat Parents

- Report them to credit agencies, so they can't borrow money for themselves when they're not taking care of their children.
- Use the Internal Revenue Service to help collect child support.
- Start a national deadbeat databank to enable law enforcement officers to track down negligent parents more easily.
- Make it a felony to cross state lines to avoid paying child support.

Women

————

NEVER BEFORE have American women had so many options—or been asked to make such difficult choices. It's
time not only to make women full partners in government, but to make government work for women.

The Bush Administration says it is committed to
women, but it has repeatedly acted against their interests.
A Clinton–Gore Administration will be different. Instead
of fighting to deprive women of their legal right to
choose, we will support the Freedom of Choice Act—not
because we are pro-abortion, but because we think certain
choices are too personal for politics.

Instead of making life-saving research a political issue,
we will let it serve American women by lifting the ban on
fetal tissue research and directing adequate resources to
women's health issues. And instead of vetoing legislation
to give Americans the right to take leave from work to
care for newborn children and sick relatives—a right enjoyed in every other major industrialized nation—we will
sign into law the Family and Medical Leave Act.

The Bush–Quayle Administration has failed to do right
by American women. We will do better.

We will:

Protect a Woman's Right to Choose

- *Sign into law the Freedom of Choice Act.* We recognize that personal privacy is a fundamental liberty guaranteed and protected by the United States Constitution; and that our government thus has no right to interfere with the difficult and intensely personal decisions women must sometimes make regarding abortion. Signing the Freedom of Choice Act will ensure that a woman's right to choose is not jeopardized by a Supreme Court reversal or limitation of *Roe v. Wade.*
- Urge Congress to *repeal the Hyde Amendment,* which prohibits federally funded abortions even for rape and incest victims.
- *Repeal President Bush's "gag" rule,* which prohibits medical personnel in federally funded clinics from advising women on pregnancy options, including abortion.
- Oppose any federal attempt to limit access to abortion through mandatory waiting periods or *parental or spousal consent* requirements; support state efforts to require some form of adult counseling or consultation for underage girls who choose to have an abortion—as long as workable and effective judicial bypass provisions are attached to such laws.
- Initiate measures to *protect women and care-givers from intimidation, harassment, and threats* posed by radical demonstrators who illegally block health clinics.
- Reduce the need for abortion by urging Congress to reauthorize the Title X Family Planning Program; by prioritizing research and development at the National Institutes of Health of safe, effective contraception; by providing *improved family planning services and educa-*

tion programs; and by ensuring the availability of contraceptives to low-income women.

Protect Women's Rights in the Workplace

• Support efforts to *ensure fair wages for all workers,* regardless of gender, and to ban gender-based discrimination in federal hiring, promotion, and contracts.
• *Hire and appoint more women* at all levels of government so that a Clinton–Gore Administration better reflects this country's population.
• Press for and enforce *tough sexual harassment guidelines* in all government agencies.

Support Pro-family and Pro-children Policies

• *Grant additional tax relief* to families with children.
• *Expand the Earned Income Tax Credit* to guarantee a "working wage" so that no American who works full-time is forced to live in poverty.
• *Sign into law the Family and Medical Leave Act,* which George Bush vetoed in 1990, so that no worker is forced to choose between maintaining his or her job and caring for a newborn child or sick family member.
• Create a *child-care network* as complete as the public school network, tailored to the needs of working families; give parents choices between competing public and private institutions.
• Establish more *rigorous standards for licensing child-care facilities* and implement improved methods for enforcing them.
• *Crack down on deadbeat parents* by reporting them

to credit agencies, so they can't borrow money for themselves when they're not taking care of their children. Use the Internal Revenue Service to collect child support, start a national deadbeat databank, and make it a felony to cross state lines to avoid paying support.

Ensure Affordable Quality Health Care for All Americans

• Provide *health coverage for all Americans* with a core benefits package that includes ambulatory physician care, inpatient hospital care, prescription drugs, basic mental health services, and important preventive programs like pre-natal care and annual mammograms.

• Sign into law the Women's Health Research Act, the Reproductive Health Equity Act, and similar legislative measures designed to *address current deficiencies in the treatment of women's health problems.*

• Use whatever means are available to find cures for diseases like ovarian cancer, breast cancer, and osteoporosis—including *lifting the fetal tissue research ban.*

• Develop a *comprehensive maternal and child health network* to reduce both the infant mortality rate and the number of low-birth-weight babies.

• Support testing of RU-486, the French birth control pill.

Crack Down on Violence Against Women

• Sign the Violence Against Women Act, which would provide *tougher enforcement and stiffer penalties to deter domestic violence.*

Appendices

The Clinton–Gore Record

In a LIFETIME spent serving the people of Arkansas, Bill Clinton has put government to work for change. His twelve years as governor have helped transform Arkansas into a national model for increasing jobs, improving education, and helping families. Working together, Bill Clinton and the people of Arkansas have created a better future for their children.

Gov. Clinton is nationally recognized as a leader in efforts to reinvent government and reform the Democratic party. He has harnessed the initiative of private citizens to the resources of public agencies, fought special interests, and turned new ideas into fast action. The people of Arkansas know Clinton serves them well. They have elected him five times, making Clinton the longest-serving governor in America. In 1991 Clinton's fellow governors voted him "the most effective governor in the nation."

It has not been easy. Gov. Clinton has had to fight interest groups every step of the way. In 1983 his education reforms met opposition from unions that didn't think teachers should have to take competency tests. Clinton fought for his initiative and won. The children of Arkansas did, too—with better instruction from their teachers and better scores for themselves.

In 1989 and 1991 Clinton took on the National Rifle Association—perhaps the single most powerful lobby in the United States—when it sponsored a law that would have prohibited gun control by local governments. As a hunter, Bill Clinton knew that Americans have a constitutional right to bear arms. But as a parent and a citizen, and as the only Southern governor ever to support the Brady Bill to provide a waiting period for the purchase of handguns, he knew that the law was wrong. He was told he'd be destroyed if he vetoed the bill. And he vetoed the bill—twice.

In 1988 Clinton fought for an Ethics and Lobbyist Disclosure Act. It required professional lobbyists to disclose the money they spent to influence public officials, and public officials to disclose information about their sources of income. Every big lobbyist in Arkansas attacked Gov. Clinton. When the legislature failed to pass the bill, Clinton took his case to the people, leading an initiative drive. The people overwhelmingly supported the initiative, and it became law.

Clinton has shown real leadership against real odds. When he first became governor, Arkansas was inadequately prepared to compete in the emerging global economy. A poor and predominantly rural state, it had begun to shift toward a non-agricultural economy in the 1950s. But by the 1970s, many of the low-wage manufacturing plants that had moved to Arkansas were shifting overseas, where costs were even lower. The state needed a leader who would act to help working people.

Bill Clinton put the state's economy back on track. By improving the local business climate, expanding opportunity in export markets, and supporting worker training and apprenticeship initiatives, he rebuilt the state's economic base and created tens of thousands of jobs. Clinton's record is outstanding: Arkansas has led all surrounding states in economic growth for several years. Because of Bill Clinton, this medium-size state now ranks second nationally in job growth and sixth in per capita income growth.

Governors with more resources but less wherewithal have created budget shortfalls and increased income taxes in just two years in office. In twelve years, Gov. Clinton transformed Arkansas's economy without doing either, balancing eleven budgets in a row and making the hard spending choices. He kept the per capita state and local tax burden the second lowest in the nation. And Clinton recently cut taxes for hundreds of thousands of middle-class Arkansans.

Nothing has been more central to Bill Clinton, or more important to the people of his state, than education. Creating growth by investing in learning and training— "putting people first"—is one of Gov. Clinton's basic commitments. Clinton has tirelessly fought for educational change, and reformers nationwide recognize him as a leader in expanding opportunity and demanding responsibility in return. In a little more than a decade, Clinton has taken one of America's worst educational systems and made it a national model for reform.

Through relentless efforts to provide Arkansas's children with a brighter future, Gov. Clinton has created a school choice program and increased teacher salaries, fought for statewide testing of students and reporting on school performance, and established a tough new curriculum and required parental involvement. Under a new program, students who drop out of school for no good reason lose their driver's licenses. Clinton's reform efforts have paid handsome dividends: at a time when the nation's students are performing poorly, Arkansas boasts rising student scores on standardized tests and the highest high school graduation rate in the region.

Gov. Clinton's efforts to improve education have gone far beyond the schoolhouse. He has developed a special bond program, approved by Arkansas voters, to help parents finance college attendance and created the Arkansas Academic Challenge Scholarships to provide college aid to middle-income and poor students who get good grades and stay off drugs. The results: the college-going rate is nearly a third higher than in 1983.

Gov. Clinton has made special efforts to help Arkansas's youngest citizens. By improving and expanding preventive medical care for pregnant mothers and young children, Clinton has cut the state's infant mortality rate almost in half since 1978. Recently he established the Better Chance Program, which sharply improves and expands state-funded early childhood programs for at-risk children aged three to five. And in yet another innovation, he has helped parents and children learn together by bringing from Israel the Home Instructional Program for Pre-school Youngsters (HIPPY). HIPPY is widely emulated across America, but Arkansas's program remains the nation's largest. In 1988, Clinton's service to children earned him one of the "Good Guy" awards from the National Women's Political Caucus.

Gov. Clinton has also put people first in Arkansas by improving health care. Against significant opposition, Clinton has launched a major effort to curb teen pregnancy, and he has fought to give local school districts the right to establish school-based health clinics. Today there are twenty-one such clinics in Arkansas, providing thousands of children with care and counseling they could not otherwise receive. Clinton has also guided into law a Health Care Access Law and a law that will make basic health coverage available for all Arkansans not currently covered by health insurance. Because of his hard work, efforts to attract doctors and retain hospitals are making progress in the Mississippi Delta, one of America's most medically underserved areas. And unlike those who have ignored the AIDS crisis, Clinton has responded clearly and decisively by forming the first working group of governors to respond to the epidemic and by establishing confidential voluntary testing in every Arkansas county.

Swift and determined response to crisis is at the heart of Clinton's leadership. In his very first term, Gov. Clinton fought against problems in the welfare system, designing legislation that expressed one of his core ideas—that government should create opportunity and demand responsibility from every citizen. In 1988 he became a driving force in the passage of the federal Family Support Act, the largest reform of welfare in history. Clinton went on to create an Arkansas welfare-to-work program, Project Success, which was one of the first such programs implemented in the country. In one year alone, it helped almost 10,000 people find work.

To help single parents, Clinton has established one of the nation's most aggressive programs to collect child support. The Arkansas Child Support Enforcement Unit has received national recognition for its success in forcing parents to take care of their kids. The unit collected $41 million in 1991, 20 percent more than in 1990. When Clinton says he will hold parents responsible, he means it.

Because of Bill Clinton, Arkansas has done more to reward people who play by the rules. But it has also cracked down on people who break the rules—dealing drugs and committing crimes. Clinton has toughened laws that punish drug and violent crime, strengthened Arkansas's prison system, and enforced the capital punishment laws of his state. His quest for innovative solutions is clear; he's developed "boot camps" that instill discipline in nonviolent first-time offenders. The recidivism rates at the camps are unusually low.

Gov. Clinton has also helped Arkansas live up to its nickname—the Natural State. It has some of the cleanest water and purest air in the nation, and Bill Clinton is part of the reason why. Under his leadership, Arkansas became one of a few states to meet all federal standards under the Clean Air Act, and the first state whose hazardous waste program was approved by the Environmental Protection Agency. Gov. Clinton has cracked down on polluters and empowered state employees with right-to-know laws. Because of his work, Arkansas was recently recognized as one of the top ten states in efforts to protect wetlands and improve energy efficiency. Arkansas agencies recently received more than a dozen awards for recycling, waste reduction, and other environmental efforts.

Clinton has done a lot more for Arkansas—creating equal opportunity, helping farmers and veterans, protecting older citizens, promoting the arts. But the story is similar in every case. Clinton has analyzed the situation, proposed new kinds of solutions, and pressed those solutions into action. Tirelessly working to challenge the status quo, Bill Clinton continues to fight for change.

Bill Clinton, a fifth-generation Arkansan, was born William Jefferson Blythe IV in Hope, Arkansas, on August 19, 1946, three months after his father died in a traffic accident. When Clinton was four years old, his mother, Virginia, married Roger Clinton, a car dealer from Hot Springs. Clinton was raised in Arkansas.

In 1968 he received a bachelor's degree from Georgetown University and went on to spend two years at Oxford University as a Rhodes Scholar. Clinton earned a law degree from Yale University Law School in 1973.

Clinton began his political career in 1974 with an unsuccessful campaign for Congress. Two years later, he was elected Attorney General. He became Governor in 1978, lost his reelection bid in 1980, but was returned to office in 1982 and has served ever since.

In 1975, Clinton married Hillary Rodham, whom he had met at Yale. She is also a lawyer and one of America's leading advocates for children. They have a daughter, Chelsea, now twelve, who is a student in the Little Rock public school system.

During sixteen years in public service representing the people of Tennessee, Al Gore has gained national recognition for his leadership, courage, and vision. He has built a reputation for hard-nosed investigation, tenacious advocacy for consumers, thorough research, and an expert's command of the subjects he tackles. On environmental issues, for example, Al Gore is recognized internationally for his leadership.

Al Gore was elected to the U.S. Senate after serving

eight years in the U.S. House of Representatives. Sen. Gore won reelection in 1990, becoming the first candidate in modern history—Republican or Democrat—to carry all ninety-five of Tennessee's counties.

The chairman of the U.S. Senate delegation to the Earth Summit—the world's largest gathering ever of heads of state—Al Gore has an environmental record that is unparalleled. He is the author of the national best-seller *Earth in the Balance: Ecology and the Human Spirit,* which outlines an international plan of action to confront the global environmental crisis. In Congress, he has introduced and advocated a broad range of environmental proposals, often introducing to Congress issues never before examined there, such as global warming.

In recent years alone, Al Gore has gained passage of measures to speed up the phase-out of ozone-depleting chemicals; introduced legislation to stop "environmental racism," which places minority communities at greater risk; and put together a historic agreement between the intelligence community and environmental scientists to make available to the civilian scientific community for the first time information about the earth gathered through intelligence efforts. Sen. Gore was the principal sponsor of the resolution establishing April 22 as Earth Day 1990 and the author of legislation to encourage recycling and strengthen markets for recycled products. Al Gore is also a key sponsor of the Strategic Environment Research Program, a groundbreaking effort to promote cooperation between military and civilian scientists and researchers to advance the efforts of both to understand the global environment.

Sen. Gore is recognized as one of the leading arms-control experts in Congress because of his mastery of the intricacies of these issues. In 1982 he introduced a landmark comprehensive arms-control plan that later became one of the central features of the U.S. negotiating position in the START talks. His pioneering proposal to eliminate land-based multiple-warhead missiles on both sides was recently adopted as the central agreement between Russia and the United States. One of ten Senate observers to the Geneva arms-control talks, Al Gore has doggedly pursued innovative thinking which coupled sharp reductions in numbers of weapons with a shift to single-warhead missiles. In addition, Sen. Gore is the author of legislation aimed at stopping the proliferation of nuclear missile technology to Third World countries. On other foreign policy issues, Al Gore has a record of strong support for the state of Israel; he supported the authorization of the use of force in the war against Iraq— and was the first to call upon the Bush Administration to recognize and respond to the plight of the Kurds after the war ended; he has been a persistent critic of U.S. policy toward the former Yugoslavia, calling for more effective efforts to stop the fighting.

Al Gore's leadership also has extended to health-care issues, where he focused attention and action on critical areas—for example, conducting hearings that led to passage of the National Organ Transplant Act, which he helped write, to establish a national network to match organ donors and recipients. He was also the lead sponsor of legislation strengthening warning labels on cigarettes and a principal backer of the measure to place warning labels on alcoholic beverages.

Al Gore's leadership on high-technology issues is reflected in his successful twelve-year effort to create a new, national, high-speed network of information "superhighways" linking America's most powerful computers with schools and research centers that otherwise would not have access to these powerful machines. Sen. Gore's High Performance Computing Act was signed into law in December 1991 and has been described as the single most important step America can take to become more competitive in the international marketplace of the future. Building on that effort, Gore has introduced the Information Infrastructure and Technology Act of 1992 to more quickly move the advanced technologies developed under the high performance computing bill to schools, health-care facilities, and industries to improve education, lower health-care costs, and create jobs. Al Gore also is the author of measures to develop and disseminate new technologies to improve manufacturing, create jobs, and protect the environment by increasing energy efficiency and developing alternative energy sources.

Recognizing that in the 1980s middle-class families paid more in taxes and worked longer hours but for less money, Sen. Al Gore became the first in the 92nd Congress to call for real tax relief for middle-income families, introducing the Gore-Downey Working Family Tax Relief Act. The legislation would increase and replace the existing personal exemption with a tax credit for children and would expand the Earned Income Tax Credit for working families with children. The legislation pays for itself by asking the wealthiest to pay their fair share.

As an advocate for consumers and taxpayers, Al Gore has taken on the cable television industry, manufacturers of contact lenses, telephone companies, and the federal government, leading investigations into the lack of quality control in the U.S. space program, government waste, inadequate nutrition, and labeling of food products and toys that are hazardous to children. Sen. Gore is also the nationwide leader in the fight to stop skyrocketing cable television rate increases, with legislation that would return to local officials the ability to regulate rate increases.

Al Gore's Senate committee assignments include Commerce, Science, and Transportation, where he is chair of the Subcommittee on Science, Technology and Space; Armed Services; Rules; and the Joint Economic Committee. He is a member of the Senate Arms Control Observer Group and the TVA Congressional Caucus.

Al Gore was born on March 31, 1948, the son of former U.S. Sen. Albert Gore, Sr., and Pauline Gore. Raised in Carthage, Tennessee, and Washington, D.C., he received a degree in government with honors from Harvard University in 1969. After graduation, he volunteered for enlistment in the U.S. Army and served in Vietnam. Returning to civilian life, Al Gore became an investigative reporter with *The Tennessean* in Nashville. He attended Vanderbilt University Divinity School and Vanderbilt Law School and operated a small homebuilding business.

Al Gore is married to the former Mary Elizabeth "Tipper" Aitcheson. They have three daughters and one son: Karenna, born August 6, 1973; Kristin, born June 5, 1977; Sarah, born January 7, 1979; and Albert III, born October 19, 1982. Gore owns a small livestock farm near Carthage, where the family lives when Congress is not in session.

Announcement Speech

Old State House
Little Rock, Arkansas
October 3, 1991

THANK YOU ALL for being here today, for your friendship and support, for giving me the opportunity to serve as your Governor for eleven years, for filling my life full of blessings beyond anything I ever deserved.

I want to thank especially Hillary and Chelsea for taking this big step in our life's journey together. Hillary, for being my wife, my friend, and my partner in our efforts to build a better future for the children and families of Arkansas and America. Chelsea, in ways she is only now coming to understand, has been our constant joy and reminder of what our public efforts are really all about: a better life for all who will work for it, a better future for the next generation.

All of you, in different ways, have brought me here today, to step beyond a life and a job I love, to make a commitment to a larger cause: preserving the American Dream . . . restoring the hopes of the forgotten middle class . . . reclaiming the future for our children.

I refuse to be part of a generation that celebrates the

death of communism abroad with the loss of the American Dream at home.

I refuse to be a part of a generation that fails to compete in the global economy and so condemns hardworking Americans to a life of struggle without reward or security.

That is why I stand here today, because I refuse to stand by and let our children become part of the first generation to do worse than their parents. I don't want my child or your child to be part of a country that's coming apart instead of coming together.

Over twenty-five years ago, I had a professor at Georgetown who taught me that America was the greatest country in history because our people believed in and acted on two simple ideas: first, that the future can be better than the present; and second, that each of us has a personal, moral responsibility to make it so.

That fundamental truth has guided my public career, and brings me here today. It is what we've devoted ourselves to here in Arkansas. I'm proud of what we've done here in Arkansas together. Proud of the work we've done to become a laboratory of democracy and innovation. And proud that we've done it without giving up the things we cherish and honor most about our way of life—solid, middle-class values of work, faith, family, individual responsibility, and community.

As I've traveled across our state, I've found that everything we believe in, everything we've fought for, is threatened by an administration that refuses to take care of our own, has turned its back on the middle class, and is afraid to change while the world is changing.

The historic events in the Soviet Union in recent months teach us an important lesson: national security begins at home. For the Soviet empire never lost to us on the field of battle. Its system rotted from the inside out, from economic, political, and spiritual failure.

To be sure, the collapse of communism requires a new national security policy. I applaud the President's recent initiative in reducing nuclear weapons. It is an important beginning. But make no mistake—the end of the Cold War is not the end of threats to America. The world is still a dangerous and uncertain place. The first and most solemn obligation of the President is to keep America strong and safe from foreign dangers and promote democracy around the world.

But we cannot build a safe and secure world unless we can first make America strong at home. It is our ability to take care of our own at home that gives us the strength to stand up for what we believe around the world.

As Governor for eleven years, working to preserve and create jobs in a global economy, I know our competition for the future is Germany and the rest of Europe, Japan and the rest of Asia. And I know that we are losing America's leadership in the world because we're losing the American Dream right here at home.

Middle-class people are spending more hours on the job, spending less time with their children, bringing home a smaller paycheck to pay more for health care and housing and education. Our streets are meaner, our families are broken, our health care is the costliest in the world and we get less for it.

The country is headed in the wrong direction fast,

slipping behind, losing our way . . . and all we have out of Washington is status quo paralysis. No vision, no action. Just neglect, selfishness, and division.

For twelve years, Republicans have tried to divide us—race against race—so we get mad at each other and not at them. They want us to look at each other across a racial divide so we don't turn and look to the White House and ask, Why are all of our incomes going down? Why are all of us losing jobs? Why are we losing our future?

Where I come from we know about race-baiting. They've used it to divide us for years. I know this tactic well and I'm not going to let them get away with it.

For twelve years, the Republicans have talked about choice without really believing in it. George Bush says he wants school choice even if it bankrupts the public schools, and yet he's more than willing to make it a crime for the women of America to exercise their individual right to choose.

For twelve years, the Republicans have been telling us that America's problems aren't their problem. They washed their hands of responsibility for the economy and education and health care and social policy and turned it over to fifty states and a thousand points of light. Well, here in Arkansas we've done our best to create jobs and educate our people. And each of us has tried to be one of those thousand points of light. But I can tell you, where there is no national vision, no national partnership, no national leadership, a thousand points of light leaves a lot of darkness.

We must provide the answers, the solutions. And we will. We're going to turn this country around and get it moving again, and we're going to fight for the hardworking middle-class families of America for a change.

Make no mistake. This election is about change: in our party, in our national leadership, and in our country.

And we're not going to get positive change just by Bush-bashing. We have to do a better job of the old-fashioned work of confronting the real problems of real people and pointing the way to a better future. That is our challenge in 1992.

Today, as we stand on the threshold of a new era, a new millennium, I believe we need a new kind of leadership, leadership committed to change. Leadership not mired in the politics of the past, not limited by old ideologies. Proven leadership that knows how to reinvent government to help solve the real problems of real people.

That is why today I am declaring my candidacy for President of the United States. Together I believe we can provide leadership that will restore the American Dream, that will fight for the forgotten middle class, that will provide more opportunity, insist on more responsibility, and create a greater sense of community for this great country.

The change we must make isn't liberal or conservative. It's both, and it's different. The small towns and main streets of America aren't like the corridors and back rooms of Washington. People out here don't care about the idle rhetoric of "left" and "right" and "liberal" and "conservative" and all the other words that have made our politics a substitute for action. These families are crying out desperately for someone who believes the promise of America is to help them with their struggle to get ahead, to offer them a green light instead of a pink slip.

This must be a campaign of ideas, not slogans. We don't need another President who doesn't know what he wants to do for America. I'm going to tell you in plain language what I intend to do as President. How we can meet the challenges we face—that's the test for all the Democratic candidates in this campaign. Americans know what we're up against. Let's show them what we're for.

We need a new covenant to rebuild America. It's just common sense. Government's responsibility is to create more opportunity. The people's responsibility is to make the most of it.

In a Clinton Administration, we are going to create opportunity for all. We've got to grow this economy, not shrink it. We need to give people incentives to make long-term investment in America and reward people who produce goods and services, not those who speculate with other people's money. We've got to invest more money in emerging technologies to help keep high-paying jobs here at home. We've got to convert from a defense to a domestic economy.

We've got to expand world trade, tear down barriers, but demand fair trade policies if we're going to provide good jobs for our people. The American people don't want to run from the world. We must meet the competition and win.

Opportunity for all means world-class skills and world-class education. We need more than "photo ops" and empty rhetoric—we need standards and accountability and excellence in education. On this issue, I'm proud to say that Arkansas has led the way.

In a Clinton Administration, students and parents and teachers will get a *real* Education President.

Opportunity for all means pre-school for every child who needs it, and an apprenticeship program for kids who don't want to go to college but do want good jobs. It means teaching everybody with a job to read, and passing a domestic GI Bill that would give every young American the chance to borrow the money necessary to go to college and ask them to pay it back either as a small percentage of their income over time or through national service as teachers or policemen or nurses or child-care workers.

In a Clinton Administration, everyone will be able to get a college loan as long as they're willing to give something back to their country in return.

Opportunity for all means reforming the health-care system to control costs, improve quality, expand preventive and long-term care, maintain consumer choice, and cover everybody. And we don't have to bankrupt the taxpayers to do it. We do have to take on the big insurance companies and health-care bureaucracies and get some real cost control into the system. I pledge to the American people that in the first year of a Clinton Administration we will present a plan to Congress and the American people to provide affordable, quality health care for all Americans.

Opportunity for all means making our cities and our streets safe from crime and drugs. Across America, citizens are banding together to take their streets and neighborhoods back. In a Clinton Administration, we'll be on their side—with new initiatives like community policing, drug treatment for those who need it, and "boot camps" for first-time offenders.

Opportunity for all means making taxes fair. I'm not out to soak the rich. I wouldn't mind being rich. But I do believe the rich should pay their fair share. For twelve years, the Republicans have raised taxes on the middle class. It's time to give the middle class tax relief.

Finally, opportunity for all means we must protect our environment and develop an energy policy that relies more on conservation and clean natural gas so all our children will inherit a world that is cleaner, safer, and more beautiful.

But hear me now. I honestly believe that if we try to do these things, we will still not solve the problems of today or move into the next century with confidence unless we do what President Kennedy did and ask every American citizen to assume personal responsibility for the future of our country.

The government owes our people more opportunity, but we all have to make the most of it through responsible citizenship.

We should insist that people move off welfare rolls and onto work rolls. We should give people on welfare the skills they need to succeed, but we should demand that everybody who can work go to work and become a productive member of society.

We should insist on the toughest possible child support enforcement. Governments don't raise children, parents do. And when they don't their children pay forever, and so do we.

And we have got to say, as we've tried to do in Arkansas, that students have a responsibility to stay in school. If you drop out for no good reason, you should lose your driver's license. But it's important to remember that the most irresponsible people of all in the 1980s were those at the top—not those who were doing worse, not the hardworking middle class, but those who sold out our savings-and-loans with bad deals and spent billions on wasteful takeovers and mergers, money that could have been spent to create better products and new jobs.

Do you know that in the 1980s, while middle-class income went down, charitable giving by working people went up? And while rich people's incomes went up, charitable giving by the wealthy went down. Why? Because our leaders had an ethic of get it while you can and to heck with everybody else.

How can you ask people who work or who are poor to behave responsibly when they know that the heads of our biggest companies raised their own pay in the last decade by four times the percentage their workers' pay went up? Three times as much as their profits went up. When they ran their companies into the ground and their employees were on the street, what did they do? They bailed out with "golden parachutes" to a cushy life. That's just wrong.

Teddy Roosevelt and Harry Truman and John Kennedy didn't hesitate to use the bully pulpit of the presidency. They changed America by standing up for what's right. When Salomon Brothers abused the Treasury markets, the President was silent. When the ripoff artists looted our S&Ls, the President was silent. In a Clinton Administration, when people sell their companies and their workers and their country down the river, they'll get called on the carpet. We're going to insist that they invest in this country and create jobs for our people.

In the 1980s, Washington failed us, too. We spent

more money on the present and the past and less on the future. We spent $500 billion to recycle assets in the S&L mess, but we couldn't afford $5 billion for unemployed workers or to give every kid in this country the chance to be in Head Start. We can do better than that, and we will.

A Clinton Administration won't spend our money on programs that don't solve problems and a government that doesn't work. I want to reinvent government to make it more efficient and more effective. I want to give citizens more choices in the services they get, and empower them to make those choices. That's what we've tried to do in Arkansas. We've balanced the budget every year and improved services. We've treated taxpayers like our customers and our bosses, because they are.

I want the American people to know that a Clinton Administration will defend our national interests abroad, put their values into our social policy at home, and spend their tax money with discipline. We'll put government back on the side of the hardworking middle-class families of America who think most of the help goes to those at the top of the ladder, some goes to the bottom, and no one speaks for them.

But we need more than new laws, new promises, or new programs. We need a new spirit of community, a sense that we are all in this together. If we have no sense of community, the American Dream will continue to wither. Our destiny is bound up with the destiny of every other American. We're all in this together, and we will rise or fall together.

A few years ago, Hillary and I visited a classroom in Los Angeles, in an area plagued by drugs and gangs. We talked to a dozen sixth graders whose number one concern was being shot going to and from school. Their second worry was turning twelve or thirteen and being forced to join a gang or be beaten. And finally, they were worried about their own parents' drug abuse.

Nearly half a century ago, I was born not far from here, in Hope, Arkansas. My mother had been widowed three months before I was born. I was raised for four years by my grandparents, while she went back to nursing school. They didn't have much money. I spent a lot of time with my great-grandparents. By any standard, they were poor. But we didn't blame other people. We took responsibility for ourselves and for each other because we knew we could do better. I was raised to believe in the American Dream, in family values, in individual responsibility, and in the obligation of government to help people who were doing the best they could.

It's a long way in America from that loving family which is embodied today in a picture on my wall in the Governor's office of me at the age of six holding my great-grandfather's hand to an America where children on the streets of our cities don't know who their grandparents are and have to worry about their own parents' drug abuse.

I tell you, by making common cause with those children we give new life to the American Dream. And that is our generation's responsibility—to form a new covenant . . . more opportunity for all, more responsibility from everyone, and a greater sense of common purpose.

I believe with all my heart that together we can make this happen. We can usher in a new era of progress, prosperity, and renewal. We can. We must. This is not just a campaign for the presidency—it is a campaign for the future, for the forgotten hardworking middle-class families of America who deserve a government that fights for them. A campaign to keep America strong at home and around the world. Join with us. I ask for your prayers, your help, your hands, and your hearts. Together we can make America great again, and build a community of hope that will inspire the world.

Vice Presidential Announcement

Remarks by Gov. Bill Clinton
and Sen. Al Gore
Governor's Mansion
Little Rock, Arkansas
July 9, 1992

WHEN I SELECTED Warren Christopher, Madeleine Kunin, and Vernon Jordan to head a team to recommend a vice presidential running mate, I asked them for a candidate who met three tests. I said I wanted a Vice President who really understood what had happened to ordinary Americans in the last twelve years, someone who was committed to making government work again for average, hardworking American families. I said I wanted a Vice President who would complement me and my own experiences and bring other experiences, knowledge, and understanding to our common endeavor. And above all, I said I wanted a Vice President who would be ready, should something happen to me, to immediately assume the office of President of the United States.

Over the last several weeks we have conducted a deliberative vice presidential search. We considered many fine, qualified candidates who have much to offer our country and this campaign. I want to express my thanks to all the outstanding men and women whom we considered and to tell you how deeply moved I was by the love and concern that each of them have for this great nation.

The running mate I have chosen is a leader of great strength, integrity, and stature. A father who, like me, loves his children and shares my hunger to turn this economy around, to change our country and to do it so that we don't raise the first generation of children to do worse than their parents.

The man standing beside me today has what it takes to lead this nation from the day we take office. Senator Al Gore of Tennessee.

Throughout his public life, Al Gore has done what I've tried to do here in Arkansas. He's put government back on the side of ordinary men and women. Time and again he's stood up to powerful interests to put people first. He's fought for health care and consumer protection. He is perhaps America's leading proponent of the development of new technologies like fiber optics and biotechnology to create the high-wage jobs America needs to move into the twenty-first century.

Like me, he's a longtime supporter of helping the working poor, and as important as anything else he has demonstrated a consistent commitment to the children of America—among other things, with our common idea to ask the wealthy in our country to pay their fair share so we can give a break to middle-class families who are trying to raise their kids in dignity and strength.

Today he is perhaps better known than anything else for his willingness and readiness, his commitment, and his ability to do something that George Bush is not willing to do: to be a leader in protecting the world's environment.

Al Gore has spent the last decade working on the global environmental challenges we desperately need to address—global warming, ozone depletion, and energy conservation. He has written a magnificent book on his thoughts and recommendations. He has asked me to join in his commitment not only to preserve the environment of America but to preserve the environment of our globe for future generations. And together we will finally give the United States a real environmental presidency.

Al Gore is a leading expert in foreign policy, national security, and arms control. He supported the use of American force to drive Saddam Hussein from Kuwait. And when the Gulf War was over, Al Gore did himself even more credit by being the one who took George Bush to task for abandoning the Kurds and shamed the Republicans for trying to use patriotism as a political issue.

Together Al Gore and I will see that America once again has a foreign policy based on American values of freedom and independence and human rights and global economic growth.

I have admired Al Gore for many years; I have admired his family, their generations of commitment to civil rights and equal opportunity to education and economic advancement for the people of our region. I know he's as proud as I am that we both are married to two of the most devoted children's advocates in the United States of America.

For in the end, Al Gore and I understand what this election is really all about—the end of years of drift and division and denial, the beginning of an honest attempt to rebuild and reunite and renew this great nation, not just for ourselves but for our children and for our children's children.

In this election Al Gore and I won't just be sharing the spot on the Democratic ticket. We'll be sharing the values we learned in Hope, Arkansas, and Carthage, Tennessee: individual responsibility, hard work, faith and family and the idea that people who work hard and live by the rules should be rewarded with the American Dream.

We want to fight against all the odds, to create jobs and raise incomes in this country again, to value our families by strengthening them in their efforts to work and to raise their children, to make government work for people again. We share a common philosophy that it's time to move beyond the old ideas of something for nothing on the one hand and every person for himself on the other. And most of all, we're ready to roll up our sleeves and get to work to move things forward in this nation.

Twelve years is long enough for a nation to have no economic strategy, no unifying vision, no common purpose. Our people are hurting and our country is slipping behind. We can't afford four more years of an administration without a plan to turn the country around, with a President and a Vice President not strong enough and determined enough to make it happen.

We have the best plan. And now we have the best ticket.

I am proud to say to all of you here and to the United States, this is the next Vice President of the United States of America, Senator Al Gore of Tennessee.

———

SENATOR AL GORE: Ladies and gentlemen, I can tell you truthfully I didn't seek this, and up until very recently when I began to get an inkling that I would get the call that came late last night, I didn't expect it.

But I'm here for one simple reason: I love my country. And I believe in my heart that this ticket gives our country the best chance for the change we so desperately need, to move forward again.

I'm proud to stand here with Bill Clinton at the beginning of a long hard fight on behalf of the hardworking people of the United States of America. We have watched for twelve long years as the Republican Administration still in power has driven this country into the ditch. The time has come for all Americans to get off the sidelines, to get involved in the process, to be a part of the healing this country needs, to bring us together, not divide us one from another, to get to work on the changes for the average working people of this country. The time has come.

Throughout American history each generation has passed on leadership to the next. That time has come again. The time for a new generation of leadership for the United States of America.

I believe very deeply that this nation simply cannot afford another four years of the kind of leadership that we have now. They've run out of ideas, they've run out of energy, they've run out of the ability to inspire our people. One of my greatest hopes as I join this ticket is to help Bill Clinton in his dramatic effort to lift the public dialogue, so that we can make this campaign a national conversation about America's future, so that we can present to the American people ideas, choices, a sensible plan for getting our country moving in the right direction again.

Bill Clinton has for his entire career stood for that kind of responsible change to improve the lives of the average people in Arkansas and in this country. I want to be a part of that effort.

I know from conversations that the two of us have had that Bill Clinton is speaking from his heart when he says here, as he did just a few minutes ago, that together we can make all the difference in determining whether or not the United States of America will offer the leadership our world needs to save the earth's environment. We're in a race against time; that leadership is critical and it can't wait four years or eight years, it can't wait any longer than November. We're going to make that change for the earth's environment and for the people of this country.

The Republican Administration has been trying to divide us for too long. They claim to be pro-family. But when we pass legislation for the people of this country which gives mothers and fathers a chance to have a little time off from work when a child is seriously injured or when a child is first born, the Bush–Quayle Administration vetoes it because they're afraid that it's going to cost money to the wealthy and powerful in this country. That's not pro-family. The Clinton–Gore ticket is the pro-family ticket in this race, and will be the pro-family Administration.

When the Democratic Congress passes an idea that Bill Clinton advanced, to give a tax credit for working families with children to make it possible for families to stay together, for families to be able to give their children the kind of upbringing that they need, the Bush–Quayle

Administration vetoes that legislation, and still tries to describe itself as pro-family.

We're going to lay out the plan that Bill Clinton has put forward. We're going to present choices to the American people. We're going to ask all Americans, regardless of what party you're in, whether you are an independent, whether you have been tempted to give up on the whole political process or not, we want you to join our team. We want you to join this common effort to bring our country together to get it moving in the right direction again.

I come from Carthage, Tennessee. I've never been to Hope, Arkansas, but I'm told that it's just like Carthage in one respect—it's a place where people know about it when you're born and care about it when you die. That's the America Bill Clinton and I grew up in. And when we elect Bill Clinton President, that's the kind of nation we will once again become.

A Vision for America

Sen. Al Gore
Democratic National Convention
New York City
July 16, 1992

LADIES AND GENTLEMEN, I have to tell you, I've been dreaming of this moment since I was a kid growing up in Tennessee, that one day I'd have the chance to come here to Madison Square Garden and be the warm-up act for Elvis.

My friends, I thank you for your confidence expressed in the vote this evening. I pledge to pour my heart and soul into this crusade on behalf of the American people. And I accept your nomination for the vice presidency of the United States of America.

I did not seek this nomination, nor did I expect it. But I am here to join this team because I love my country and because I believe in my heart that together Bill Clinton and I offer the American people the best chance we have as a nation to move forward in the right direction again.

I'm here because the country I love has a government that is failing our people—failing the forgotten majority in your hometown and mine—those who scrimp and save and work hard all their lives to build a better life for their children.

I'm here to renew a journey our founders began more than 200 years ago. In my lifetime I have seen America's ideals and dreams change the world. And I believe that now is the time to bring those ideals and dreams home, here, to change America.

Our country is in trouble. And while George Bush and Dan Quayle have been making excuses for deadlock and delay, people in other nations inspired by the eternal promise of America have torn down the Berlin Wall, brought communism to its knees, and forced a racist government in South Africa to turn away from apartheid.

Throughout the world, obstacles to liberty that many thought might stand forever turned out to simply be no match for men and women who decided in their hearts that their future could be much greater than their past would let them dream. Their faith in the power of conscience and their confidence in the force of truth required a leap of the human spirit.

Can we say truthfully that their chance for change was better than ours? And yet we face our own crisis of the spirit here and now in America. We're told we can no longer change; we've seen our better days. They even say we're history.

The cynics are having a field day because across this country millions of American families have been betrayed by a government out of touch with our values and beholden to the privileged few.

Millions of people are losing faith in the very idea of democracy and are even in danger of losing heart because they feel their lives may no longer have any deeper meaning or purpose. But you can't kill hope that easily, not in America, not here where a cynic is just a disappointed idealist in disguise, a dreamer yearning to dream again.

In every American, no matter how badly betrayed or poorly led, there is always hope. Even now, if you listen, you can hear the pulse of America's true spirit. No, the American spirit isn't gone. But we vow here tonight that in November George Bush and Dan Quayle will be history.

I'm not saying that they're bad people. But their approach to governing this country has badly failed. They have taxed the many to enrich the few. And it is time for them to go.

They have given us false choices, bad choices, and no choice. And it is time for them to go.

They have ignored the suffering of those who are victims of AIDS, of crime, of poverty, of ignorance, of hatred, and harassment. It is time for them to go.

They have nourished and appeased tyranny and endangered America's deepest interests while betraying our cherished ideals. It is time for them to go.

They have mortgaged our children's future to avoid the decisions they lack the courage to make. It is time for them to go.

They embarrassed our nation when the whole world was asking for American leadership in confronting the environmental crisis. It is time for them to go.

They have demeaned our democracy with the politics of distraction, denial, and despair. What time is it?

CROWD: *It's time for them to go.*

———

What time is it?

CROWD: *It's time for them to go.*

What time is it?

CROWD: *It's time for them to go.*

The American people are disgusted with excuses and tired of blame. They know that throughout American history each generation has passed on leadership to the next. That time has come again. The time for a new generation of leadership for the United States of America to take over from George Bush and Dan Quayle. And you know what that means for them. It's time for them to go.

Ladies and gentlemen, in 1992 our challenge is not to elect the last President of the twentieth century but to elect the first President of the twenty-first century, President Bill Clinton.

Bill Clinton has a plan that offers real answers for the real problems of real people. A bold new economic strategy to rebuild this country and put our people back to work.

And if you want to know what Bill Clinton can do, take a look at what he has already done. For more than a decade he has been fighting against incredible odds to bring good jobs, better skills, and genuine hope to one of the poorest states in our country.

A decade ago when his state needed dramatic reform to shake up one of the poorest school systems in America, Bill Clinton took on the established interests and made

Arkansas the first state to require teacher testing. He has cut classroom size, raised test scores above the national average, and earned the support of both teachers and parents who now know Bill Clinton will be the real Education President for this country.

For most of the last decade, while the Republicans have been trying to use welfare to divide us, Bill Clinton has led the fight to reform the welfare system, to move people off welfare and into the workforce. And he did all this while balancing eleven budgets in a row.

Let me say that again: while balancing eleven budgets in a row and giving the people of Arkansas one of the lowest tax burdens in this country. No wonder Arkansas under Bill Clinton has been creating manufacturing jobs at ten times the national rate. And no wonder that when all of the nation's governors, Republicans and Democrats alike, were asked to vote on who was the most effective governor in all the land, by an overwhelming margin they chose Bill Clinton.

What we need in America in 1992 is a President who will unleash the best in us by putting faith in the decency and good judgment of our people—a President who will challenge us to be true to our values and examine the ways in which our own attitudes are sometimes barriers to the progress we seek. I'm convinced that America is ready to be inspired and lifted again by leaders committed to seeking out the best in our society, developing it and strengthening it.

I've spent much of my career working to protect the environment, not only because it is vital to the future of my state of Tennessee, our country, and our earth and air, but because I believe there is a fundamental link between our current relationship to the earth and the attitudes that stand in the way of human progress.

For generations we have believed that we could abuse the earth because we were somehow not really connected to it. But now we must face the truth. The task of saving the earth's environment must and will become the central organizing principle of the post–Cold War world.

And just as the false assumption that we are not connected to the earth has led to the ecological crisis, so the equally false assumption that we are not connected to each other has led to our social crisis.

Even worse, the evil and mistaken assumption that we have no connection to those generations preceding us or those who will follow us has led to the crisis of values we face today. Those are the connections that are missing from our politics today. Those are the bridges we must rebuild if we are to rebuild our country. And those are the values we must honor if we are to recapture the faith in the future that has always been the heart of the American Dream.

We have another challenge as well. In the wake of the Cold War and in the reemergence of ancient ethnic and racial hatreds throughout the world, the United States must once again prove that there is a better way.

Just as we accepted as a people, on behalf of all humankind, the historic mission of proving that political freedom is the best form of government, and that economic freedom is the best engine of prosperity, we must now accept the obligation of proving that freedom from prejudice is the heart and soul of community—that, yes, we can get along.

Yes, people of all backgrounds can not only live together peacefully but enrich one another, celebrate diversity, and come together as one. Yes, we will be one people—and live the dream that will make this world great.

In the end, this election isn't about politics. It isn't
even about winning, though that's what we're going to
do. This election is about the responsibilities that we owe
one another—the responsibilities we owe our children—
the calling we hear to serve our country, and to be a part
of a community larger than ourselves.

You've heard a lot in the past week about how much
Bill Clinton and I have in common. Indeed, we both
share the values we learned in our hometowns—individual responsibility, faith, family, and the belief that hard
work should be rewarded. We're both fathers with young
children—children who are part of a generation whose
very future is very much at stake in this election. And
we're both proud of our wives, Hillary Clinton and Tipper
Gore, two women who have done more for the children
of this country in the last twelve years than the last two
men who have sat in the Oval Office have done in their
entire lifetimes.

I'm proud my father and mother could be here tonight
to see me join a ticket that will make good on the best
advice they ever gave me: to tell the truth and always love
my country. My sister and I were born to two wonderful
people who worked hard to give us a better life.

Nineteen ninety-two is the Year of the Woman. It's
also the forty-sixth anniversary of the year my mother,
born in a time when women weren't even allowed to vote,
became one of the first women to graduate from Vanderbilt Law School.

My father was a teacher in a one-room school who worked his way to the United States Senate. I was eight years old when my father's name was placed in nomination for the vice presidency before the Democratic Convention in 1956. And growing up, I watched him stand courageously for civil rights, economic opportunity, and a government that worked for ordinary people.

I don't know what it's like to lose a father. But I know what it's like to lose a sister, and almost lose a son. I wish my late sister, Nancy, could be here this evening. But I am grateful beyond words for the blessings that my family has shared.

Three years ago my son, Albert, was struck by a car crossing the street after watching a baseball game in Baltimore. Tipper and I watched as he was thrown thirty feet through the air and scraped another twenty feet on the pavement after he hit the ground.

I ran to his side and held him and called his name, but he was limp and still, without breath or pulse. His eyes were open with the empty stare of death. And we prayed, the two of us, there in the gutter, with only my voice. His injuries inside and out were massive. And for terrible days he lingered between life and death. Tipper and I spent the next thirty days and nights there at his bedside.

Our family was lifted and healed in no small measure by an incredible outpouring of love and compassion and prayers from thousands and thousands of people, most of whom we never even knew.

Albert is plenty brave and strong, and with the support of three wonderful sisters, Karenna, Kristin, and Sarah, and two loving parents who helped him with his exercises every morning and prayed for him every night, he pulled through. And now, thank God, he has fully recovered and runs and plays and torments his older sisters like any little boy.

But, ladies and gentlemen, I want to tell you this straight from my heart—that experience changed me forever. When you've seen your six-year-old son fighting for his life, you realize that some things matter a lot more than winning. You lose patience with the lazy assumption of so many in politics that we can always just muddle through. When you've seen your reflection in the empty stare of a boy waiting for his second breath of life, you realize that we were not put here on earth to look out for our needs alone.

We are part of something much larger than ourselves. All of us are part of something much greater than we are capable of imagining. And, my friends, if you look up for a moment from the rush of your daily lives, you will hear the quiet voices of your country crying out for help. You will see your reflection in the weary eyes of those who are losing hope in America. And you will see that our democracy is lying there in the gutter waiting for us to give it a second breath of life.

I don't care what party you're in, whether you're an independent, whether you have been tempted to just give up completely on the whole political process, we want you to join this common effort to unite our country behind a higher calling.

If you have been supporting Ross Perot, I want to make a special plea to you this evening: stay involved. You have already changed politics in this country for the better; keep on fighting for change.

The time has come for all Americans to be a part of

the healing. In the words of the Bible, do not lose heart. This nation will be renewed.

In order to renew our nation, we must renew ourselves. Just as America has always transcended the hopes and dreams of every other nation on earth, so must we transcend ourselves. And in Gandhi's words, "Become the change we wish to see in the world."

Let those of us alive today resolve with one another that we will so conduct ourselves in this campaign and in our lives that 200 years from now Americans will say of our labors that this nation and this earth were healed by people they never even knew.

I'm told that Hope, Arkansas, is indeed a lot like my hometown, Carthage, Tennessee—a place where people do know about it when you're born and care about it when you die. That's the America Bill Clinton and I grew up in. That's the kind of nation we want our children to grow up in. Just as Hope is a community, so is America.

When we bring the community of America together we will rekindle the American spirit and renew this nation for generations to come. And the way to begin is to elect Bill Clinton President of the United States of America.

A New Covenant

Gov. Bill Clinton
Democratic National Convention
New York City
July 16, 1992

My fellow Americans, tonight I want to talk with you about my hope for the future, my faith in the American people, and my vision of the kind of country we can build, together.

I salute the good men who were my companions on the campaign trail: Tom Harkin, Bob Kerrey, Doug Wilder, Jerry Brown, and Paul Tsongas. One sentence in the platform we built says it all: "The most important family policy, urban policy, labor policy, minority policy, and foreign policy America can have is an expanding, entrepreneurial economy of high-wage, high-skill jobs."

And so, in the name of all the people who do the work, pay the taxes, raise the kids, and play by the rules, in the name of the hardworking Americans who make up our forgotten middle class, I accept your nomination for President of the United States.

I am a product of that middle class. And when I am President you will be forgotten no more.

We meet at a special moment in history, you and I. The Cold War is over; Soviet communism has collapsed; and our values—freedom, democracy, individual rights, and free enterprise—have triumphed all around the world. And yet just as we have won the Cold War abroad, we are losing the battles for economic opportunity and social justice here at home. Now that we have changed the world, it's time to change America.

I have news for the forces of greed and the defenders of the status quo: your time has come—and gone. It's time for a change in America.

Tonight ten million of our fellow Americans are out of work. Tens of millions more work harder for lower pay. The incumbent President says unemployment always goes up a little before a recovery begins. But unemployment only has to go up by one more person before a *real* recovery can begin. And, Mr. President, you are that man.

This election is about putting power back in *your* hands and putting government back on *your* side. It's about putting people first.

You know, I've said that all across the country, and someone always comes back at me, as a young man did just this week at the Henry Street Settlement on the Lower East Side of Manhattan. He said, "That sounds good, Bill. But you're a politician. Why should I trust you?"

Tonight, as plainly as I can, I want to tell you who I am, what I believe, and where I want to lead America.

I never met my father. He was killed in a car wreck on a rainy road three months before I was born, driving home from Chicago to Arkansas to see my mother.

After that, my mother had to support us. So we lived with my grandparents while she went back to Louisiana to study nursing.

I can still see her clearly tonight through the eyes of a three-year-old: kneeling at the railroad station and weeping as she put me back on the train to Arkansas with my grandmother. She endured her pain because she knew her sacrifice was the only way she could support me and give me a better life.

My mother taught me. She taught me about family and hard work and sacrifice. She held steady through tragedy after tragedy. And she held our family, my brother and me, together through tough times. As a child, I watched her go off to work each day at a time when it wasn't always easy to be a working mother.

As an adult, I've watched her fight off breast cancer. And again she has taught me a lesson in courage. And always, always she taught me to fight.

That's why I'll fight to create high-paying jobs so that parents can afford to raise their children today. That's why I'm so committed to making sure every American gets the health care that saved my mother's life, and that women's health care gets the same attention as men's. That's why I'll fight to make sure women in this country receive respect and dignity—whether they work in the home, out of the home, or both. You want to know where I get my fighting spirit? It all started with my mother.

Thank you, Mother. I love you.

When I think about opportunity for all Americans, I think about my grandfather.

He ran a country store in our little town of Hope. There were no food stamps back then. So when his customers, whether they were white or black, who worked hard and did the best they could, came in with no money—well, he gave them food anyway. Just made a note of it. So did I. Before I was big enough to see over the counter, I learned from him to look up to people other folks looked down on.

My grandfather just had a grade-school education. But in that country store he taught me more about equality in the eyes of the Lord than all my professors at George-town; more about the intrinsic worth of every individual than all the philosophers at Oxford; and he taught me more about the need for equal justice than all the jurists at Yale Law School.

If you want to know where I come by the passionate commitment I have to bringing people together without regard to race, it all started with my grandfather.

I learned a lot from another person, too. A person who for more than twenty years has worked hard to help our children—paying the price of time to make sure our schools don't fail them. Someone who traveled our state for a year, studying, learning, listening, going to PTA meetings, school board meetings, town hall meetings, putting together a package of school reforms recognized around the nation, and doing it all while building a distinguished legal career and being a wonderful, loving mother.

That person is my wife.

Hillary taught me. She taught me that all children can learn, and that each of us has a duty to help them do it. So if you want to know why I care so much about our children and our future, it all started with Hillary. I love you.

Frankly, I'm fed up with politicians in Washington lecturing the rest of us about "family values." Our families *have* values. But our government doesn't.

I want an America where "family values" live in our actions, not just in our speeches. An America that includes every family, every traditional family and every extended family, every two-parent family, every single-parent family, and every foster family—every family.

I do want to say something to the fathers in this country who have chosen to abandon their children by neglecting to pay their child support: take responsibility for your children or we will force you to do so. Because governments don't raise children; parents do. And you should.

And I want to say something to every child in America tonight who is out there trying to grow up without a father or a mother: I *know* how you feel. You're special, too. You matter to America. And don't ever let anybody tell you you can't become whatever you want to be. And if other politicians make you feel like you're not a part of their family, come on and be part of ours.

The thing that makes me angriest about what's gone wrong in the last twelve years is that our government has lost touch with our values, while our politicians continue to shout about them. I'm tired of it.

I was raised to believe that the American Dream was built on rewarding hard work. But we have seen the folks in Washington turn the American ethic on its head. For too long, those who play by the rules and keep the faith have gotten the shaft, and those who cut corners and cut deals have been rewarded. People are working harder than ever, spending less time with their children, working nights and weekends at their jobs instead of going to PTA and Little League or Scouts, and their incomes are still going down. Their taxes are going up, and the costs of health care, housing, and education are going through the roof. Meanwhile, more and more of our best people are falling into poverty—even when they work forty hours a week.

Our people are pleading for change, but government is in the way. It has been hijacked by privileged, private interests. It has forgotten who really pays the bills around here—it's taking more of your money and giving you less in return.

We have *got* to go beyond the brain-dead politics in Washington, and give our people the kind of government they deserve: a government that works for them.

A President ought to be a powerful force for progress. But right now I know how President Lincoln felt when General McClellan wouldn't attack in the Civil War. He asked him, "If you're not going to use your army, may I borrow it?" And so I say, George Bush, if you won't use your power to help America, step aside. I will.

Our country is falling behind. The President is caught in the grip of a failed economic theory. We have gone from first to thirteenth in the world in wages since Reagan and Bush have been in office. Four years ago, *candidate* Bush said America is a special place, not just "another pleasant country on the U.N. roll call, between Albania and Zimbabwe." Now, under *President* Bush, America has an unpleasant economy stuck somewhere between Germany and Sri Lanka. And for most Americans, Mr. President, life's a lot less kind and a lot less gentle than it was before your Administration took office.

Our country has fallen so far, so fast that just a few

months ago the Japanese Prime Minister actually said he felt "sympathy" for the United States. Sympathy. When I am your President, the rest of the world will not look down on us with pity, but up to us with respect again.

What is George Bush doing about our economic problems? Now, four years ago he promised us fifteen million new jobs by this time. And he's over fourteen million short. Al Gore and I can do better.

He has *raised* taxes on the people driving pickup trucks, and *lowered* taxes on people riding in limousines. We can do better.

He promised to balance the budget, but he hasn't even tried. In fact, the budgets he has submitted have nearly doubled the debt. Even worse, he *wasted* billions and reduced our investment in education and jobs. We can do better.

So if you are sick and tired of a government that doesn't work to create jobs; if you're sick and tired of a tax system that's stacked against you; if you're sick and tired of exploding debt and reduced investments in our future—or if, like the great civil rights pioneer Fannie Lou Hamer, you're just plain old sick and tired of being sick and tired—then *join* us, *work* with us, *win* with us. And we can make our country the country it was meant to be.

Now, George Bush talks a good game. But he has no game plan to rebuild America from the cities to the suburbs to the countryside so that we can compete and win again in the global economy. I do.

He won't take on the big insurance companies and the bureaucracies to control health costs and give us affordable health care for all Americans. But I will.

He won't even implement the recommendations of his own commission on AIDS. But I will.

He won't streamline the federal government, and change the way it works; cut 100,000 bureaucrats, and put 100,000 new police officers on the streets of American cities. But I will.

He has never balanced a government budget. But I have, eleven times.

He won't break the stranglehold the special interests have on our elections and the lobbyists have on our government. But I will.

He won't give mothers and fathers the simple chance to take some time off from work when a baby is born or a parent is sick. But I will.

We're losing our family farms at a rapid rate, and he has no commitment to keep family farms in the family. But I do.

He's talked a lot about drugs, but he hasn't helped people on the front line to wage that war on drugs and crime. But I will.

He won't take the lead in protecting the environment and creating new jobs in environmental technology. But I will.

You know what else? He doesn't have Al Gore. And I do. Just in case you didn't notice, that's Gore with an *e* on the end.

And George Bush won't guarantee a woman's right to choose. I will. Listen, hear me now: I am not pro-abortion. I am pro-choice strongly. I believe this difficult and painful decision should be left to the women of America. I hope the right to privacy can be protected and we will never again have to discuss this issue on political platforms. But I am old enough to remember what it was like before *Roe v. Wade.* And I do not want to return to the time when we made criminals of women and their doctors.

Jobs. Education. Health care. These are not just commitments from my lips. They are the work of my life.

Our priorities must be clear: we will put our people first again. But priorities without a clear plan of action are just empty words. To turn our rhetoric into reality we've got to change the way government does business—fundamentally. Until we do, we'll continue to pour billions of dollars down the drain.

The Republicans have *campaigned* against big government for a generation. But have you noticed? They've *run* this big government for a generation. And they haven't changed a thing. They don't want to fix government. They still want to campaign against it, and that's all.

But, my fellow Democrats, it's time for us to realize that we've got some changing to do, too. There is not a program in government for every problem. And if we want to use government to help people, we've got to make it work again.

Because we are committed in this convention and in this platform to making these changes, we are, as Democrats, in the words that Ross Perot himself spoke today, a revitalized Democratic party. I am well aware that all those millions of people who rallied to Ross Perot's cause wanted to be in an army of patriots for change. Tonight I say to them: join us and together we will revitalize America.

Now, I don't have all the answers. But I do know the old ways don't work. Trickle-down economics has sure failed. And big bureaucracies, both private and public, they've failed, too.

That's why we need a new approach to government—a government that offers more empowerment and less entitlement, more choices for young people in the schools they attend, in the public schools they attend, and more choices for the elderly and for people with disabilities and the long-term care they receive—a government that is leaner, not meaner. A government that expands opportunity, not bureaucracy—a government that understands that jobs must come from growth in a vibrant and vital system of free enterprise. I call this approach a New Covenant—a solemn agreement between the people and their government, based not simply on what each of us can take but on what all of us must give to our nation.

We offer our people a new choice based on old values. We offer opportunity. We demand responsibility. We will build an American community again. The choice we offer is not conservative or liberal. In many ways it's not even Republican or Democratic. It's different. It's new. And it will work.

It will work because it is rooted in the vision and the values of the American people. Of all the things George Bush has ever said that I disagree with, perhaps the thing that bothers me most is how he derides and degrades the American tradition of seeing—and seeking—a better future. He mocks it as "the vision thing." But remember just what the Scripture says: "Where there is no vision the people perish."

I hope nobody in this great hall tonight or in our beloved country has to go through tomorrow without a vision. I hope no one ever tries to raise a child without a vision. I hope nobody ever starts a business or plants a crop in the ground without a vision—for where there is no vision the people perish.

One of the reasons we have so many children in so much trouble in so many places in this nation is because they have seen so little opportunity, so little responsibility, and so little loving, caring community that they literally cannot imagine the life we are calling them to lead. And so I say again, where there is no vision America will perish.

What is the vision of our New Covenant?

An America with millions of new jobs in dozens of new industries moving confidently toward the twenty-first century. An America that says to entrepreneurs and business people: we will give you more incentives and more opportunity than ever before to develop the skills of your workers and create American jobs and American wealth in the new global economy. But you must do your part: you must be responsible. American companies must act like American companies again—exporting products, not jobs. That's what this New Covenant is all about.

An America in which the doors of college are thrown open once again to the sons and daughters of stenographers and steelworkers. We'll say: everybody can borrow the money to go to college. But you must do your part. You must pay it back—from your paychecks, or better yet, by going back home and serving your communities. Just think of it: millions of energetic young men and women, serving their country by policing the streets, or teaching the children or caring for the sick, or working with the elderly or people with disabilities, or helping young people to stay off drugs and out of gangs, giving us all a sense of new hope and limitless possibilities. That's what this New Covenant is all about.

An America in which health care is a right, not a privilege. In which we say to all of our people: your government has the courage—finally—to take on the health-care profiteers and make health care affordable for every family. But you must do your part: preventive care, pre-natal care, childhood immunization; saving lives, saving money, saving families from heartbreak. That's what the New Covenant is all about.

An America in which middle-class *incomes*—not middle-class taxes—are going up. An America, yes, in which the wealthiest few—those making over $200,000 a year—are asked to pay their fair share. An America in which the rich are not soaked—but the middle class is not drowned either. Responsibility starts at the top; that's what the New Covenant is all about.

An America where we end welfare as we know it. We will say to those on welfare: you will have and you deserve the opportunity through training and education, through child care and medical coverage, to liberate yourself. But then, when you can, you must work, because welfare should be a second chance, not a way of life. That's what the New Covenant is all about.

An America with the world's strongest defense; ready and willing to use force, when necessary. An America at the forefront of the global effort to preserve and protect our common environment—and promoting global growth. An America that will not coddle tyrants, from Baghdad to Beijing. An America that champions the cause of freedom and democracy, from Eastern Europe to

Southern Africa, and in our own hemisphere in Haiti and Cuba.

The end of the Cold War permits us to reduce defense spending while still maintaining the strongest defense in the world. But we must plow back every dollar of defense cuts into building American jobs right here at home. I know well that the world needs a strong America, but we have learned that strength begins at home.

But the New Covenant is about more than opportunities and responsibilities for you and your families. It's also about our common community. Tonight every one of you knows deep in your heart that we are too divided.

It is time to heal America. And so we must say to every American: look beyond the stereotypes that blind us. We need each other. All of us, we need each other. We don't have a person to waste. And yet, for too long, politicians have told the most of us that are doing all right that what's really wrong with America is the rest of us. *Them.* Them the minorities. Them the liberals. Them the poor. Them the homeless. Them the people with disabilities. Them the gays. We've gotten to where we've nearly them'd ourselves to death. Them, and them, and them. But this is America. There is no them; there is only us. One nation, under God, indivisible, with liberty, and justice, for all.

That is *our* Pledge of Allegiance, and that's what the New Covenant is all about.

How do I know we can come together to make change happen? Because I have seen it in my own state. In Arkansas we're working together and we're making progress. No, there is no Arkansas miracle. But there are a lot of miraculous people. And because of them, our schools are better, our wages are higher, our factories are busier, our water is cleaner, and our budget is balanced. We're moving ahead.

I wish I could say the same thing about America under the incumbent President. He took the richest country in the world and brought it down. We took one of the poorest states in America and lifted it up.

And so I say to those who would criticize Arkansas: come on down. Especially if you're from Washington— come to Arkansas. You'll see us struggling against some problems we haven't solved yet. But you'll also see a lot of great people doing amazing things. And you might even learn a thing or two.

In the end, the New Covenant simply asks us all to be Americans again—old-fashioned Americans for a new time. Opportunity. Responsibility. Community. When we pull together, America will pull ahead.

Throughout the whole history of this country, we have seen time and again that when we are united, we are unstoppable. We can seize this moment, we can make it exciting and energizing and heroic to be an American again. We can renew our faith in ourselves and each other, and restore our sense of unity and community. Scripture says, our eyes have not yet seen, nor our ears heard, nor our minds imagined what we can build.

But I cannot do it alone. No President can. We must do it together. It won't be easy and it won't be quick. We didn't get into this mess overnight, and we won't get out of it overnight. But we can do it—with our commitment and our creativity and our diversity and our strength. I want every person in this hall and every citizen in this land to reach out and join us in a great new adventure to chart a bold new future.

As a teenager I heard John Kennedy's summons to citizenship. And then, as a student at Georgetown, I heard that call clarified by a professor I had named Carroll Quigley, who said America was the greatest country in the history of the world because our people have always believed in two great ideas: first, that tomorrow can be better than today, and second, that each of us has a personal, moral responsibility to make it so.

That future entered my life the night our daughter, Chelsea, was born. As I stood in that delivery room, I was overcome with the thought that God had given me a blessing my own father never knew: the chance to hold my child in my arms.

Somewhere at this very moment, another child is born in America. Let it be our cause to give that child a happy home, a healthy family, a hopeful future. Let it be our cause to see that child reach the fullest of her God-given abilities. Let it be our cause that she grow up strong and secure, braced by her challenges, but never, never struggling alone; with family and friends and a faith that in America no one is left out; no one is left behind.

Let it be our cause that when she is able, she gives something back to her children, her community, and her country. And let it be our cause to give her a country that's coming together, and moving ahead—a country of boundless hopes and endless dreams; a country that once again lifts up its people and inspires the world.

Let that be our cause and our commitment and our New Covenant.

I end tonight where it all began for me: I still believe in a place called Hope.